DOGMA

by Michael Schmaus

4 *The Church: Its Origin and Structure*

Translated by Mary Ledderer

SHEED AND WARD: NEW YORK

Library of Congress Cataloging in Publication Data

Schmaus, Michael, 1897–
  Dogma.

  "A project of John XXIII Institute, Saint Xavier
College, Chicago."
  Translation of Der Glaube der Kirche.
  Includes bibliographical references.
  CONTENTS: v. 1. God in revelation.—v. 2. God
and creation.—v. 3. God and His Christ. [etc.]
  1. Theology, Doctrinal. I. John XXIII Institute,
Chicago.
BT75.2.S3513   230.2   68-26033
ISBN 0-8362-0496-4 (v. 4)

Nihil Obstat: Leo J. Steady, Ph.D., S.T.D. & Thomas J. Beary, Ph.D.,
              Censors Librorum
Imprimatur: + John A. Marshall, *Bishop of Burlington*
July 24, 1972

iv

Contents

Contents

Introduction

Jesus Christ is the representative of God among men. In him God is present in history and in all of creation. He is also the representative of men before God. He was this during his earthly life; he remained this after his death and will continue to be this through eternity. As representative of men before God, he led in his historical existence an earthly life measured to sinful man, without himself being sinful. This life found its highest expression in his death on Golgotha in the name of mankind. The presence of God in Jesus assumed its highest expression in his resurrection. It is the risen Christ who is the true representative of God among men.

There is no other man in history whose life has had such immeasurable effects as the life of Jesus. The Epistle to the Hebrews expresses this idea by saying that Jesus died, once for all, a saving death in the name of all mankind (Heb. 9,26f.).

The statement that Jesus died this saving death only once for all time does not sufficiently characterize its scope. It is, however, of the greatest significance, for it lifts the saving death of Jesus out of the realm of the mythical savior. For believers in myth, the death of the mythical god repeats itself like an event of nature in recurring cycles. The universal saving character of the death of Jesus is grounded in the fact that he died once for all time and need not die again. For this reason there is no other name given to men whereby they can achieve salvation (Acts 4,12); there is no other way to salvation except Jesus (Jn. 14,6). The dying of Jesus, once for all time, together with his resurrection, is implanted within history—the past which lay behind him and the future following upon his earthly life—as a new, inner, saving mystery. Jesus' life, all his activity, but especially his death and resurrection, have eschatological—that is, final—significance, shaping the entire future to come.

But the Christ-event, happening once, at a definite time and place, does not work automatically like a law of nature or with the momentum of a historical force. Jesus confronts every man with the decision whether he will accept him as his representative before God, and as God's representative to him. Although Jesus possesses universal significance, that is, for all of mankind, nevertheless every single man is individually asked the question, for man is that being who is capable of being asked and of giving an answer.

Jesus is the general *a priori* of all individual destinies. In him and through him God has given himself to humankind. But here arises the difficult and fundamental problem as to how such a confrontation can take place with a Jesus who lived at a particular time and in a specific geographic place. We must eliminate the answer of myth: that it occurs through a repetition in the present of that which took place then and there. We must also exclude the narrowly intellectualized answer that it occurs through the recollection of that event. The first answer maintains too much, the second too little. Scripture, tradition, Church teaching and theological reflection all admit only one answer: it occurs through the dynamic making-present of that event in every generation. The actual making-present produces at any given time a contemporaneity between the Savior and his salvation on the one hand and those in need of salvation or those represented by the Savior on the other hand.

We can arrive at a similar solution by another route. Jesus is God's final word of salvation to mankind. But what happened in the land of Palestine, on Golgotha, on Easter morning, in the sending of the Spirit, is not yet full and complete salvation. It is the source of salvation, and it is that in a final sense, so that we cannot reckon with any other source or ground of salvation. This source, however, is ordered toward the future participation of man. Only when all men, or those ultimately called by God to salvation, participate in the events of that time, in faith, in baptism, will that final salvation ripen fully into the completeness of salvation. Until then salvation is final in its source, but still incomplete in its fulfillment, which is to say, in its appropriation, which latter is of course not to be understood as purely a work of man, but rather as worked by God and then appropriated through a free decision of man for Christ. That the salvation brought by Christ possesses finality in this sense, we know by faith. This situation, however, will only become clear when the finality develops into fulfillment. (Cf. here the work of M. Boutin soon to be published: "Untersuchung über die Eschatologie R. Bultmanns.")

How is it brought about that something which happened in the past is now made present? Through the Word. It will become evident that this statement, that salvation is made present through the Word, not only does not exclude, but strengthens the role of the sacrament, inasmuch as the sacrament is a special form of the Word. The Word, however, presupposes a community, for it must have a speaker and a hearer. Christ did not leave to the chance of human encounter the bringing of salvation through the Word. Instead he provided for it by preparing a community which would serve this purpose. This community is the Church. The Church has, accordingly, the function of making present something and someone of the past. This is a temporal activity. What happens in time, however, happens necessarily also in space. The temporal problem of making salvation present leads us of necessity, then, to the question, Where does this occur? The Christian answer again is: In the Church. The Church is the instrument by which God makes salvation present and at the same time the place where he does so. The salvation-event of Jesus Christ is made present in and through the Church, which means that Jesus Christ is present in the Church as the One forever marked with his death and resurrection. Jesus Christ is present in the Church in that he is made present by her word; or better, he makes himself present and accessible through the word of the Church, which is his instrument in virtue of the activity of the Holy Spirit. The Church is thus both an eschatological community of believers gathered around Jesus Christ and, at the same time, the instrument commissioned by him to assist men to salvation.

This community which we call "the Church" exists on a number of levels. It is christocentric, and it can be understood only if this is taken into account. But this leads us further. In Jesus, God the Father is present: we saw that Jesus must be understood as the original sacrament; that all his words and deeds, even up to his death on the cross and resurrection, are sacramental events, even if they embody sacramentality in different degrees. If Jesus is present, then the God he represents is present. As a result the Church itself has a sacramental character; however, its sacramentality is derived and secondary. The seven sacraments as we know them are to be understood as particular forms of the total sacramentality of the Church expressing itself in particular situations in the life of the Church and of the individual believer. Furthermore, as Jesus during his earthly life performed every saving action in the Spirit, so also he is present in the Church through his Spirit. So we must consider this aspect of the Church too, its function as the dwelling place of the Spirit (pneumatological aspect), together with the christological and sacramental aspects.

The presence of the Christ-event in the Church and through the Church continues until the end of time. When the end-time comes, the Church will cease to be an instrument of man's salvation. Because God's gift of himself to man, although it is given once and for all and definitively at its source, brings fulfilled salvation only in the future, the Church as the instrument of God's saving design has an eschatological character. As a human society, the Church is always threatened by the temptation to want to rule rather than to serve. It must therefore, in constant repentance and self-reflection, ever be conscious of the meaning of its existence and its task of service. It is a church of perpetual self-reform.

Hence, whatever happens in the Church serves to make Christ's salvation dynamically present in the world, so that it may be appropriated by each generation. Since this is accomplished through a community, some sort of structure or organization is required, which implies an element of religious authority and corresponding subordination. The Christ-event, made present in and through the Church, takes root in the individual through human relationships. Some of these relationships result from the nature and function of the community which Christ left behind him. We must not attempt to separate the hidden grace from the visible mediating instrument of that grace.

In the exposition in this volume and the volume to follow it, the Church will be discussed from the viewpoints sketched above: the christological, the pneumatological, the structural, the sacramental, and the eschatological. All these elements are closely allied. None has ever been completely overlooked in the theological attempts to understand the Church, but they have been very differently accented from time to time.

Before we proceed to the presentation itself, a word should be said about the question whether ecclesiology, the investigation of the nature of the Church, does not belong at the beginning of a treatise on dogmatic theology. Ecclesiology would appear to be the precondition and foundation of every theological statement, for it is from the Church that we receive the Scripture which gives witness to Jesus Christ. Here there arises an unsolvable antinomy. Although it is true that ecclesiology is the foundation of all dogmatic exposition, it is just as true that the Church can only be understood from the viewpoint of Christ and his works. We are caught here in a circle; not, however, a "vicious" circle, but a circle of life. The theologian cannot speak theologically of Jesus without having before him constantly the horizon of the faith of the Church. However, he does not need to preface his christological exposition with a formal statement of his faith in the Church. The antinomy can only be bypassed by an arbitrary decision. When ecclesiology is not placed at the beginning, as a starting point for theological exposition, but is treated rather as the conclusion to Christology, then the intention is obviously to accent as strongly as possible the christocentric character of the ecclesiology. And the attendant disadvantage must be taken in the bargain.

◄ I

The Church
a Mystery of Faith

◄ 1

The Word "Church"

First of all, a word about the expression "church" itself, its derivation and meaning. The Germanic word "church" (*Kirche, Kirk*) stems from a popular Greek word, *kyriake* ("house of God"), which in turn comes from *kyriakon* ("house of the master"). The word common in the romance languages, *ecclesia*, is a Greek word taken over in the Greek translation of the Old Testament (Septuagint) from a Hebrew expression *qahal Jahweh*. It has a threefold level of meaning: in the profane use of the word, *ekklesia* means the act of assembling and the assembled community itself; in addition, however, it designates the total community of the People of God. The word "synagogue" designates the Israelite place of community assembly. The New Testament designation, *ecclesia*, means also the new, the true Israel, and not simply the existing community but the act of assembling the community and the assembled community. It has therefore the sense of an occurrence, an act, as well as an institutional meaning. How far the profane use of the word influenced the biblical it is difficult to decide. In any case, a basic distinction is involved—namely, that in the profane use, the word *ekklesia* refers to the assembly of all the free citizens of the state, summoned by the proclamation of the herald to make decisions on legal or political questions. In the Scriptures, however, the word means a coming together not only of men but also of women and children, not for the purpose of decision-making, but for the obedient acceptance of a decision already made, a judgment handed down from God—for receiving the holy word of God.

The word *ekklesia* is used in the different books of the New Testament with varying frequency. We do not find it at all in Mark, Luke, John; in the second letter to Timothy; the letter to Titus; the two letters of Peter; the two letters of John; or the letter of Jude. In Matthew it occurs three times (Mt. 16,18; 18,17), in Revelation thirteen times, in the letter of James once (5,14). The expression is found frequently in the Acts and in the letters of Paul. The first reference in the Acts of the Apostles is to the church in Jerusalem (Acts 2,47; 8,1.3). Then the word refers also to the church in Judea, in Galilee, and in Samaria (Acts 9,31). Thus in the beginning what was spoken of was not "the churches" but "the church" in the singular. In Acts the word means not only the local congregation but also the totality of the congregations, which does not mean a summing up of the individual communities, but rather the whole Church in each individual community. The dominant concept is of the universal Church. The original community in Jerusalem considered itself, when the Jewish people as a whole did not accept the Christian message, as the true and proper People of God, as the true Israel. The word *ekklesia* thus denotes first of all the Church of Jesus Christ formed in Jerusalem, which was in the first days the whole of the Church. As other Christian communities arose outside Jerusalem, they were included in the Church of Jerusalem. They belonged to the one Church, whose "homeland" was in Jerusalem. Jerusalem was the Mother Church. From there the designation was transferred to every Christian community.

It is noteworthy that the Acts frequently appends to the word *ekklesia* the expression *tou theou* ("of God"; cf. Acts 20,28). This addition points to the fact that it is God who calls the community together and is present in it. It is clear from earlier statements that this God is not to be understood as the trinitarian God, but as God the Father, the first divine person. Interestingly, in the Acts of the Apostles the Church is never called the Church of Christ. This may have as its basis the fact that the word *ekklesia tou theou* is taken over from the Old Testament and ostensibly should express the fact that the believers in Christ represent the legitimate heirs of the Old Testament People of God.

In the Pauline epistles we meet the expression *ekklesia* in the same sense as in Acts. Paul also uses it for the local congregation and for the whole Church. Frequently the two meanings are interwoven. Thus Paul speaks, for instance, of the Church of God which is in Corinth or in Thessalonica or in Galatia (see the titles of the letters to these communities; also Rom. 1,7; Col. 1,2; Phil. 1,1). There are consequently, according to Paul, many churches (1 Thess. 2,14; 1 Cor. 4,17; 11,16; 16,1; 2 Cor. 8,1). Although numerically this application to the individual churches predominates, the primary meaning for him is of the whole Church as a unity (Gal. 1,13; 1 Cor. 10,32; 12,28; 15,9; Phil. 3,6). This is evident especially in the letters to the Ephesians and the Colossians. The universal Church is made manifest in the individual churches (cf. 2 Cor. 11,2). Many times also Paul adds the genitive *tou theou* and thereby makes clear that he understands the Church as the successor to the Old Testament People of God (1 Thess. 2,14; 2 Thess. 1,4; 1 Cor. 1,1; 10,32; 11,16.22). He goes beyond the terminology of Acts insofar as he frequently applies the formula "in Christ" or the genitive "of Christ," which for him says the same thing as the characteristic formula *en Christo* (1 Thess. 1,2; 2,14; 2 Thess 1,1; Gal. 1,22; Rom. 6,16). This nuance brings out more clearly than in Acts the progress from the Old Testament to the New Testament People of God, without losing the continuity. It is Christ who forms the new People of God and impresses on it its special character.

The early Church has, besides the word *ekklesia*, a list of other designations, among the most important of which are: Body of Christ, the Disciples, the Saints (Acts 9,13.32.41; 26,10; Rom. 15,25f. 31; 1 Cor. 6,1; 2 Cor. 8,4; 9,1.12), the Poor, the Believers, the Elect (Rom. 8,33; Col. 3,12; 2 Tim. 2,10; 1 Pet. 1,1; 2,9), the Brethren, the Called (Rom. 1,16; 1 Cor. 1,24; cf. Rom. 1,7; 1 Cor. 1,2), the true Israel, Israel of God, Israel in the Spirit, the sons of Abraham, the People of God, House of God, Temple of God, the Chosen People, the Servant of God, the Strangers, the Pilgrims. Each one brings a particular aspect of the Church to light; all, however, proclaim that what is under consideration is a community of men who are bound together through God's salvific initiative.

‹ 2

The Church a Mystery

Beyond all the semantic problems, the thing which we designate by the word "church" represents a mystery of the self-communication of God through Christ to the human community and thereby to individual human beings, as well as the mystery of this society itself fashioned by God's self-communication. The Church is an element of the mystery of Jesus Christ, indeed of the trinitarian God himself. It would, of course, be an exaggeration to identify the Church with Jesus Christ. That would lead to an error comparable to the monophysitism of the early Church. The Church is not simply the evolutionary form of Jesus Christ. It is, on the one hand, a mystery of the divine summons to man through Jesus Christ in the Holy Spirit; on the other hand, a mystery of man's free decision. Christ and the Church are more than Christ alone. To say otherwise would be to undervalue the human decision. But our thesis must not be equated with the statement: the Logos and creation are more than the Logos alone; for it is not the Logos that is spoken of here, but the Logos-made-flesh.

As a result of its character as mystery, the Church eludes definition in a rigorous sense. Besides, such a definition, to be complete, would have to include all the elements prominent in the progress of the Church's historical life, including its future form, which we cannot yet know.

Theological reflection upon the nature of the Church begins,

6

after some preliminary attempts, at the end of the twelfth century. At that time the overriding concern was the relationship between papal power and the power of the king. However, it is only in our own time that the Church has offered a definitive interpretation of herself (after an only partially successful beginning at the First Vatican Council). This late development may perhaps be accounted for, if not justified, by the fact that like most human societies the Church begins to take stock of itself only to the extent that its operation is impeded. The Second Vatican Council also refrained from giving a definition of the Church. It offers various descriptions in connection with the Scriptures without bringing these together in a unified concept. The Council, however, has a guiding image of itself when it makes the concept of the Church as the "People of God" the foundation of its exposition. The use of this idea constitutes a major difference between the pronouncement of the Second Vatican Council and the encyclical *Mystici Corporis* of Pius XII, in which the idea of the Church as the Body of Christ is made the foundation of all ecclesiology. But this distinction should not be understood as an essential opposition. Both expressions occur in Scripture. They are related to each other in a unity of tension. It is a question of different emphasis, or of different perspectives, rather than of different doctrine. Even though this is not made explicit by the Second Vatican Council, actually the concept of the Church as the Body of Christ is implied in the concept of the People of God. The image of the Body of Christ expresses the specific difference between the Old and New Testament People of God, while the concept of the Church as the People of God accents the continuity between the old and new covenant. Further, this latter concept is capable of bringing out more strongly the personal element in the Church, and thus is closer to that growing esteem for the person which has become one of the characteristics of our age. It has a more democratic orientation, without actually characterizing the Church as a democracy.

The Council has accepted, then, neither the well-known definition of Robert Bellarmine nor that of Johann Adam Moehler. The first, whose intent is to define membership in the Church rather than the Church itself, states (*De eccl. mil.*,2): "The Church is a union of men who are bound together through the confession of the same Christian faith and through participation in the same sacraments under the guidance of legitimate pastors, above all of the one vicar of Christ on earth, the Roman Pontiff." According to the second definition, the Church is the Son of God perpetually appearing in human form among men, always renewing himself, eternally regenerating; his enduring incarnation; for the Christian faithful are called in Holy Scripture the Body of Christ (*Symbolik*, Paragraph 36). The first definition does not state that the Church is of divine origin, while the second is in danger of being a christocentric mysticism.

Inasmuch as the Church is the beginning and the instrument of the reign of God—the kingdom of God is present in her really, dynamically, as a hidden seed—one can attempt the following description: the Church is the People of God of the New Testament, living and acting as the Body of Christ, which stands in the service of the lordship of God and the salvation of man.

Since the Church is a mystery, it is an object of faith. One can make many statements about it with insights gained from scientific and prescientific disciplines, by means of phenomenological observation, of historical research, of psychological analysis, of scientific study of religion, and the like. But what the Church really is, is revealed only to the believer. It is important, therefore, to understand rightly the phrase "faith in the Church." We must make a distinction, one first made by Augustine and since generally accepted in theology (*Tract. in Joann.*,29,6). Augustine distinguishes faith in God from faith on account of God, and from the believing acceptance of a truth communicated and guaranteed by God (*credere in deum, credere deo, credere deum*). In the first sense, faith is to be understood as a personal encounter with God, in which man gives himself into the hands of God. This faith is related to love. It is not merely an intellectual affirmation of a statement, but a personal surrender to God. Affirmation of truth is not excluded from this faith; however, it has its basis elsewhere. When we speak of faith in the Church, however, we mean that the Church is an object of faith. This can be seen in the Apostles' Creed and all the other creeds, when first of all faith in God the Father is expressed, then in God the Son, then in the Holy Spirit, and in connection with this, faith in the Church (DS 1–70).[1]

[1]Denzinger-Schönmetzer, *Enchiridion Symbolorum, Definitionum et Declarationum de Rebus Fidei et Morum* (Freiburg: Herder, 1965³³); hereafter cited as DS.

◄ II

The Church of Christ and the Church of the Spirit

There is no genuine Christology without ecclesiology, since Christ is ordained to humanity, to gather it around himself as the ground and center of its salvation. There is no ecclesiology without Christology, since Christ is the source of the Church's life and its Lord. Our understanding of the Church must derive from Christ, not from the general idea of a society. The christological view embraces two levels: that of origin and that of existence. Christ is the origin of the Church and at the same time the continuing ground of its life and its existence. Since he is this as the Glorified One, on the level of the Spirit, the Church of Christ must be considered also as the Church of the Spirit.

◄ 3

Jesus Christ the Origin of the Church

THE OLD TESTAMENT PEOPLE OF GOD AND THE INTENTION OF JESUS TO FOUND A CHURCH

Today there is general agreement that the Church in some way goes back to Christ, but the question remains open as to the way in which the Church comes from him. In contemporary Protestant theology (e.g., W. G. Kümmel) the view is common that after the shock of the crucifixion, the disciples came together again on account of the Easter experience and the descent of the Spirit, and that Jesus had actually anticipated this, but that it was completely outside his intention for the disciples to consider themselves as an eschatological community of salvation in contradistinction to the people of Israel. That Jesus himself had no intention to found a church is argued from the evidence that he expected the kingdom of God to come soon, and further from the fact that he thought of himself as sent only to the lost sons of the house of Israel (Mt. 10,8). The passage in Matthew so often cited as proof of Jesus' intention to found a church (Mt. 16,18—the promise of primacy) is subject to serious questioning. Other Protestant theologians (e.g., K. L. Schmidt, A. Oepke, O. Cullmann) differ from the Catholic viewpoint in that whereas they

13

acknowledge a precedence of the apostle Peter over the other disciples, they reject the idea of a succession to his position.

In opposition to this opinion that Jesus could have had no intention to found a church, it must be pointed out that Jesus had reckoned with a longer period of time between his death and the full coming of the kingdom of God, as we pointed out in Volume II; and further, that the cited passage from Matthew's gospel (16,18) is by no means the chief proof that Jesus intended to found a church. Yet it must be admitted that Jesus in fact knew himself to be sent to proclaim the message of salvation to the entire people of Israel, and only to them. It was not his intention to form a special group within the whole people, like the Pharisees or the Qumran community. It is also true that during the earthly life of Jesus there was no church. This was only formed at the time of, and on the basis of, the Easter and Pentecost experience. During his earthly existence Jesus had prepared for the Church by his life, by his words, and by his actions, but he had not constituted it.

The preparation consisted in setting up the individual elements which formed the foundation for the development of the Church, and in giving that promise which would be fulfilled through the constituting of the Church. Had the Old Testament People of God accepted the salvation message of Jesus, then that renewal of the old covenant would have taken place which had been foretold in many ways by the prophets (e.g., Jer. 31,31). Then it would not only have held true that salvation comes from the Jews (Jn. 4,6) but that its lasting home remains with them. Jesus' intention to create a new community of salvation distinct from the Old Testament People of God first began to appear as it became evident that his mission of salvation would miscarry and be a scandal to the people, that the fate of death lay before him. Such a thesis implies that Jesus did not always have the course of his life and his destiny clearly conceptualized in his consciousness. (This question was discussed in Volume III.) On the contrary, during the course of his life he had to listen uninterruptedly to the commissions of his heavenly Father and to actualize them in the light of his consciousness on the basis of the development of his own existence. He did not live out his life like an actor playing a role for which the script is written, which he knows in advance and has only to play through. Hence the activities of his life which prepared for the Church were occasioned by the rejection of his message by the Jews.

In the light of this consideration, the calling of the disciples and the election of the Twelve need not necessarily be viewed as actions whose intention is the formation of a church. Rather they represent, primarily, the attempt to have the saving message of the reign of God carried to the Jewish cities and villages by means of special messengers. In this way the renewal of the covenant promised by the prophets was to be carried out. However, the calling of the disciples and of the Twelve took on another intention and function as the rejection of faith by the Jews crystallized more and more clearly.

The Old Testament covenant had for a long time—in fact, from the very beginning—been endangered by the human partner to the bond. It had an extremely troubled history. It was established, according to the Torah, in historical stages—in the covenant with Noah, in that with Abraham, and in that with Moses. The covenant is a gracious gift of God. Abraham became the ancestor of the twelve tribes of Israel.

After being freed from Egypt, the tribes of Israel were finally constituted as one nation. The law of the covenant was proclaimed and accepted. The meal of the covenant was added (Ex. 24,1f.9ff.). The decisive thing was that God, although he was the God of all nations, would be in a special way the God of Israel, and Israel would be his people. As a consequence the people of Israel acquired a difficult, indeed an almost impossible, burden: they were not to be a nation in the same way as other nations but were to have a special task which consisted in this, to worship the true God and proclaim him to all the other peoples (Ex. 20,3–23). It is understandable that such a national life was not easy, that the temptation to live as other nations did was ever present, that the people fell away from God again and again, even in the first hours of their election and of being constituted as God's people; that, in the face of political, economic, cultural, and military powers of the surrounding territories, Israel did not rely on the protection of God, but rather trusted to the same kind of power with which their enemies met them. But this very failure to trust in him called forth the judgment of God. From the eighth to the fourth centuries, the prophets sent by God pointed out the consequences of such behavior, showed the judgments of God, and at the same time promised the grace of God if the people would return again to the covenant. They foretold a new covenant, but without revealing its concrete form exactly (Jer. 31,31-34; Hos. 2,20f.; Ezek. 37,15-19; Is. 54,11-15; Is. 26,19f.; Ezek. 40-48; Is. 53,3f.).

Until the activity of Jesus, the form of the new covenant remained an open question. In the writings of the New Testament we learn that Jesus is the representative of the covenant, coming forth from the Old Testament People of God. For he came in order to confirm the promises made to the patriarchs (Rom. 15,8; Eph. 3,6; Gal. 5,13; Mk. 1,15; Acts 2,36; 13,32f.; 26,16; Heb. 8,8; etc.).

He was, however, rejected by Israel. He who knew himself as Messiah was a messiah without a people. He had to form a new messianic people. The Messiah had to prepare, for the Father who had sent him, a new people, since he could not carry out his mission to the old. In this context the community forming itself around Jesus, by dissociation from its former ethnic roots, achieves a universal significance. It was to become the matrix of a new People of God in the spirit. God's plans are irrevocable. The rejection of the Messiah by the Jews cannot make illusory the promises given to Abraham (Rom. 9,6). The unfaithfulness of man cannot undermine the faithfulness of God (Rom. 3,3; 11,29). God's covenantal will must be carried on through history to the appointed goal of salvation. A new People of God must take over the historical mission of Israel. A new community of salvation, which should accept the calling addressed to Abraham, became the true seed of Abraham, the posterity of Abraham in the spirit, so that they could call Abraham father (Rom. 4,12-16; 9,6-13; Gal. 4,20).

God's call went to the Gentiles. But it was the bond which began in Abraham and received its seal in Moses into which the Gentiles were called. The God who called them was the God of Abraham, of Isaac, and of Jacob (Mk. 12,26). The Gentiles—from east and west, from north and south—will sit at table with

Abraham, Isaac, and Jacob in the kingdom of God (Mt. 8,11f.; Lk. 13,28f.). In the future, salvation should no longer be bound to a national identity. While until then the decisive dividing line had run between nations, henceforth the line should run between the baptized and unbaptized. A common blood could not remain the basis for salvation. However, precisely for that reason, the Jewish people are not shut out entirely from the covenant. A "remnant" is left (Rom. 9; cf. Is.1,9; 8,14; 10,22f.; 28,16). This remainder of the former People of God and the newly called Gentiles will together form the new People of God, will constitute the Church. And so the continuity with God's covenant established in Abraham is not broken.

At the same time, however, there is a profound difference. The new order brings with it a dissolution of that unity between religious and political life which was characteristic of the Old Testament People of God. Yet this discontinuity is superimposed on, and accomplished through, continuity. It is in the same love, in all the phases of the covenant, that God turns toward man.

THE FOUNDING OF THE CHURCH

In a mysterious divine dialectic, which is a scandal for both Jews and Gentiles, the execution of Jesus, the rejection by the People of God of the Messiah sent from God, becomes the very foundation of the new mankind, of the new bearers of the covenant of man with God. The death of Jesus was vicarious for Israel and all mankind (Gal. 3,13; 1 Cor. 11,24; 2 Cor. 5,14.21; Rom. 5,6-8; 8,34).

On the basis of the ever clearer rejection of the Messiah, the gathering of the disciples and the choice of the Twelve took on new significance. But more, Christ also began activity in direct preparation for the Church. The most important of these acts was the establishment of the communal meal, which he did on the occasion of his last meal with his disciples before his death. Also of fundamental importance is the promise given to Peter. From this context, in retrospect over the whole life of Jesus, all that he was and did and said gains a new light of orientation to the Church. This will be pointed out along several lines.

*Incarnation, Death, Resurrection, and Sending
of the Spirit as Foundation of the Church*

The incarnation of the Word and the course of his life—in particular, of course, his death, his resurrection, and the sending of the Spirit—are fundamental for the foundation of the Church. It would be a narrow interpretation to view the Church only in terms of the incarnation, or only of the death, or only of the sending of the Spirit. Rather the whole life of Jesus, the Word made flesh, forms the foundation for the establishment of the Church. One cannot separate these individual phases in the salvation-event that bears the name of Jesus Christ. They form a salvific unity, as they form a natural whole.

Since Jesus was the central cosmic idea of God, and therefore had a real relation not only to his own time and the future time after him but also to the time preceding him, it is understandable that some of the Fathers of the Church see a prefiguring of the Church already in the time before Christ. This is evidenced when they speak of the Church "from the beginning," or "from Abel onwards," or when they recognize in the Church an image of the realm of spirits brought forth by God before the visible creation. We saw earlier that the self-utterance of God which is gathered up in the personal interior Word of God was from all eternity directed to the Incarnation. We can fill out the thesis thus, that the divine self-utterance intended from eternity the gathering of men around the incarnate Logos, not in the form of a repeated hypostatic union, but in a mysterious union with the Logos become man, with the brotherly representative of all men before God—a union which is usually called mystic because it is not expressible in philosophical categories. To describe this analogically, the phrase "brotherhood with Christ" suggests itself. Thus the final origin of the Church lies in God-without-origin. The Church, like the incarnation of the Logos, and against this background the whole of creation, constitutes a theme in the eternal divine self-utterance—that is, in the dialogue of love between Father and Son which is completed in the Holy Spirit as the divine We.

Another idea must be introduced with particular reference to the Holy Spirit: the Logos-made-man accomplished his life and

death in the Holy Spirit. In the resurrection he became a
Spirit-penetrated being. As such he "sent" the spirit down upon
the community of his followers. So he is himself present in the
Church in the Holy Spirit.

The Church is, therefore, the work of the triune God in the
sense that it was created by the Trinity, by God the Father
through the Son in the Holy Spirit; but also, however, in the sense
that it reflects and participates in the tripersonal life of God. The
cause of its own unity is in the unity of God (that is, according to
Greek theology, in the Father as the source without beginning;
according to the Latin interpretation, in the unity of God's
essence); and the cause and prototype of its inner multiformity
lies in the tripersonal nature of God (cf. Eph. 1,1-5; Constitution
on the Church, 4; Decree on Ecumenism, 2). We could say that
in the Greek trinitarian view the Church lives in the movement
toward God the Father, through the incarnate Logos, in the Holy
Spirit as the personal climate of love which determines the
atmosphere of the People of the heavenly Father. In this view the
Church is always an event, as often as it goes beyond itself to
God in word and deed. Speaking concretely, according to the
Greek conception of the Trinity, the bishop is the figure of the
Father dispensing salvation; the multiplicity of priests and people
is the figure of Jesus Christ as the representative of all; the love
uniting all is an image of the Holy Spirit.

In considering the role of the incarnate Logos in the origin of
the Church, we must start from the fact that with him a new
mankind begins. The first Adam, to use a phrase from the apostle
Paul, was the progenitor of the human race which fell under the
power of sin. Jesus, the second Adam, became the progenitor of a
humanity freed from sin, death and law unto freedom and love
(1 Cor. 15,22.45.47; Rom. 5,12-21; Lk. 3,38). He became the first
of men who could and should live in peace with God and peace
with one another. The Fathers have epitomized this thesis in the
statement that in Jesus himself there was already given a whole
new humanity. He is the whole Man, the Man intended by God, in
whom the kingdom of God and the new creation are realized. This
thesis is connected with the proposition held by most of the
Fathers that Christ had assumed humanity in general (the *as-
sumptus homo* theory). In this theology the man Jesus is already,

in a quite real sense, the whole of mankind, insofar as he contains it in himself. The Church—that is, the people gathered around Jesus and believing in him—is in this conception the unfolding in time of all that is contained in Jesus. If such theses seem tinged with gnostic thinking, they do make evident what the concern of the Fathers was: Jesus is explained as the beginning of a new epoch. Irenaeus attempts to make these associations plausible with his teaching of the recapitulation of mankind in Jesus Christ. Augustine repeats the opinion of Irenaeus. The incarnation of God in the man Jesus is for him necessarily a union of God with the whole body of humanity, so that all participate in the life and activity of Jesus as the Head. The incarnation is not to be narrowly interpreted as a single event in a moment of time; it must be conceived of dynamically as the fulfillment of the whole human life of Jesus. The Fathers of the Church frequently express the meaning of the death of Jesus for the formation of the Church through the image of the Church's being born out of the wound in Jesus' side.

It would not be doing justice to the witness which the New Testament gives to the establishment of the Church, or to the theology of the Fathers, to maintain that the Church was born of itself out of the common faith of Jesus' disciples in his salvific death and resurrection, or else merely out of the will of the disciples to remain together. Actually the life of Jesus is the ontological foundation for the establishment of the Church. However, his positive intention to found a Church is also fundamental, not only for the concrete form the Church was and is to take but for its very constitution. On the ontological foundation of the incarnation, death, and resurrection arises, as it were, the actual intention of Jesus to found a church. This finds its most real expression in the sending of the Spirit. But here it must be repeated that the will of Jesus was directed first of all to the renewal of the Old Testament People of God; it was only toward the end of his public ministry, in the realization of their rejection of faith, that he turned toward an eschatological society which would be continuous with this People, yet at the same time distinct from it.

◄ 4

Preparation for the Church

THE EUCHARIST

In this chapter we will consider the most important acts by which Jesus, toward the end of his life, prepared for the Church. The primary one is the celebration of the farewell meal which was to be forever commemorated by his followers. We give particular emphasis to this memorial meal because it was destined to become the heart and center of the future life of the Church, and also because in it are united all the other acts by which Jesus prepared for the Church (cf., e.g., K. Schelkle).

On the evening before his execution Jesus met with the Twelve for the usual paschal celebration, that is, for the meal commemorating the departure from Egypt and the institution of the covenant at Sinai. If we should accept the opinion of many theologians that this eucharistic meal was not the Jewish Passover meal but an ordinary Jewish festive meal, it would not substantially alter the account, although a part of the symbolism would be lost. According to Luke (22,18), Jesus opens the meal with the assurance that he will not celebrate the paschal meal with his followers again until it is fulfilled in the "kingdom of God." He has in mind that time when the kingdom of God will no longer be hidden, but God will openly exercise his saving dominion over all men and over the whole of creation. The death which he approaches and now solemnly anticipates with his followers, and the resurrection inseparably connected with it, will put the final seal on the end of the former covenant and on the beginning of a new one. At the farewell meal on the night of his passion, the celebration of this end and this new beginning was anticipated. Jesus invited to this only the Twelve, the innermost circle who were always with him. Every meal is a symbol of brotherly communion, but the farewell meal celebrated by Jesus with his apostles realized this meaning in a deep and unique way. For he did not merely share the same table with his followers as brothers, he gave himself to them as food. His words: "Take and eat, this is my body; take and drink, this is my blood," mean nothing else than that he gives himself to his followers in an unconditional way. They could receive him so intimately in faith that they became one with him and with one another in a brotherhood unknown before. Until now, they had indeed been united in spirit, but on that night they became, as it were, blood relations. In that hour they became one body, truly one body in Jesus. Paul expresses this at one point with the words "Because there is one loaf, we, many as we are, are one body" (1 Cor. 10,17).[1] In giving himself to his followers in the symbol of the meal, in the symbol of bread and wine, Jesus showed that he would give himself to them in an intimacy and intensity that could not be exceeded. It is important to note that Jesus speaks of the body which is to be broken and of the blood which is to be shed, thus indicating that his whole existence is an unconditional surrender to the Father in the name of all men, and at the same time an unconditional surrender to mankind itself.

We may assume that the farewell meal of Jesus before his death, if it was not itself a Passover meal, nevertheless took place in the context of the Jewish Passover meal. This Jewish Easter meal, as we have noted, was a memorial meal, commemorating the exodus from Egypt and the establishment of the covenant at Sinai, both events of fundamental importance in the founding of the Old Testament People of God. But in the course of this

[1]Unless it is otherwise indicated, the excerpts quoted from the New Testament are taken from *The New English Bible, New Testament.* © The Delegates of the Oxford University Press and the Syndics of Cambridge University Press 1961. Reprinted by permission.

memorial meal Christ now basically altered its meaning. He spoke of a "new testament," making it clear that God on his own initiative, with his eternally free salvific will, intended to establish a new covenant in place of the former one. As the old covenant was sealed with blood, so is the new covenant also sealed with the sacrificial blood of Jesus Christ himself. With these words of Jesus the former era of salvation came to an end and a new era dawned. What took place in the room of the Lord's supper had epochal significance for human salvation. This meal was at the same time the last to be celebrated legitimately as a memorial meal of the old covenant and the first to be celebrated in the new order. So Jesus' farewell meal can be called the founding assembly of the Church. The meal preceding the exodus from Egypt was the sign of a departure. Jesus' farewell meal is the sign of a new departure, toward a liberation from another slavery than the former one from which God had through Moses freed the Israelite tribes. This was a departure out of the slavery of sin, and at the same time a movement away from the former covenant of God; it was the beginning of a new migration of the People of God through the desert of tribulation and affliction toward that distant but absolute future where the kingdom of God will break through in all its splendor.

Jesus' word here is of special importance, "Do this in remembrance of me" (1 Cor. 11,24f.). He foresees a long time in which he will not be visibly present with his followers (Mk. 2,20) but will nevertheless be present in that his memory will be celebrated, not in empty reminiscences but by a word filled with reality. He will remain with his followers until the end of time as the One who sacrificed himself and by his resurrection inaugurated the new and eternal life. But in so doing, he does not want merely to be present as the glorified Lord; rather he desires to give himself to his followers in continual sanctifying activity. The celebration of this memorial meal will essentially differentiate the new believers from the former People of God, who continue in their old cult. It is this memorial meal which marks the new era and is to be characteristic of the new People of God, even though it may be celebrated by individual Christian congregations with varying frequency and intensity.

This celebration is the basis of all the functions of the apostles and their successors: to sanctify, to teach, and to govern. It is at the heart of the eschatological existence of the Church. Its future celebration was the object of the calling of the disciples, and especially of the selection of the Twelve. Even though the small flock of new believers continue for a while to participate in the cult of the old order, still the new is expressed in the celebration held in their homes, and especially in the longing cry which accompanies their memorial celebration, "Marana tha" (1 Cor. 16,22). The memorial celebration was in fact not only to recall the memory of the departed Lord, but at the same time to keep alive the hope and longing for his return. In it the vision turns with greater intensity from the past toward the future. The future is celebrated in anticipation; it gives the ultimate meaning to each celebration.

Corresponding to the new order which is characterized by the celebration of this meal, there is also a new law of the covenant, namely the commandment of love. Those gathered around the one table for the celebration of their Lord's memorial are to be united in love among themselves, in that same charity in which the love of the Lord is itself represented and active. We can suppose that Jesus' parting words, reported in the characteristic Johannine formulation, are to be understood in connection with the farewell meal and are an exposition of that which was introduced by it (Jn. 14-17).

THE CALLING OF THE DISCIPLES
AND OF THE TWELVE

Now we shall attempt to describe the other acts by which Jesus founded the Church, keeping in mind that they cannot be understood apart from the context of the Eucharist. At this point once again we have to refer to the calling of the disciples and the appointing of the Twelve. The call to discipleship (Mk. 1,16-20; Mt. 4,18-22; Lk. 5,1-1; 10,11-2) is reminiscent of the call of those men of the old covenant to whom God entrusted special missions (Abraham, Moses, the prophets), especially of the appointment of the seventy helpers who received of the spirit of Moses. In contrast to other teachers, Jesus himself chose his disciples. He did not bind them to a particular tradition or school, as did the rabbis with their followers, but to his person; so they should not be called students, but rather disciples, called to a lasting community with him.

The selection of the Twelve, probably from the circle of the "disciples," was one of the most important and most consequential events of Jesus' public ministry (Mk. 3,13-19; Mt. 10,1-4; Lk. 6,12-16). The Twelve, moreover, are often called the disciples, the twelve disciples or apostles (e.g., 1 Cor. 15,5; Jn. 6,67, and the synoptic tradition). Neither the time of the calling nor the other concrete details can be historically fixed. The choice of the Twelve came entirely from Jesus' initiative. He alone determined who was to be a part of that circle. Those called into the circle of the Twelve were in no way prepared beforehand. The importance which Jesus himself attached to this act can be seen in his prayerful preparation for it. This small circle of truly devoted followers, who stayed with Jesus in constant fellowship after the spiritual leaders of Judaism had rejected him and the enthusiasm of the multitude had abated and turned into hostility, are to be initiated into the mysteries of the kingdom of God (Mk. 3,34). To them alone Jesus discloses the messianic mystery. The predictions of his passion and the instructions concerning true discipleship were intended only for them (Mk. 8,31; 9,30f.; 10,32f.; Mt. 10,5-33). It has already been pointed out that they alone were permitted to celebrate the last meal with the Lord. To be sure, even they were slow to comprehend what Jesus had to announce (Mt. 8,17f.; 8,32f.; 9,10; Mk. 4,40f.; 6,50-52; 9,5-7.34; 10,24; 10,38-41; 14,37-50). Even after the resurrection they confused the kingdom of God with an earthly kingdom in which there are worldly positions of honor (Mk. 10,35-37; Lk. 24,21; Acts 1,6).

The number twelve had a special symbolic significance in the ancient East. It was particularly sacred to the Israelites because of the twelve patriarchs and the twelve tribes descended from them (Mt. 19,28; Acts 26,7). For Israel, the people of twelve tribes, the selection of the Twelve is reminiscent of the twelve patriarchs, a symbol of Israel, and at the same time a sign of fulfillment. For the restoration of the twelve tribes was expected of the messianic age. As a result of the rejection of Jesus they appeared, however, as the symbolic prefiguring of the new People of God, as the patriarchs of the new messianic community of salvation. When Jesus chooses twelve, he implies that now the time has come when a new twelve tribes, a restored Israel, is to arise.

The significance of the number twelve became clearly apparent in the betrayal of Judas, when, after his suicide, the number had to be completed once again. Jesus sent out his chosen disciples and his appointed Twelve to proclaim the kingdom of heaven, to heal the sick, to raise the dead, to cleanse the lepers, and to drive out the demons (Mk. 6,7-13; Mt. 10,5-8; Lk. 9,1-6). This initial mission was confined to the house and the people of Israel. When those sent had discharged their commission, they returned to Jesus and reported what they had taught and done.

THE TERM "APOSTLE"

It is a secondary consideration whether Jesus himself gave to the Twelve the name "apostles," emissaries, or whether the designation comes from Luke or from the tradition of the apostolic age (Lk. 6,13; 9,10; 22,14; 24,10; but cf. also Lk. 9,1.12; 18,31; 22,3; 22,47; Acts 6,2). What is important is that the Twelve from the beginning constituted a "college," a community called and commissioned for special service (cf. Mk. 3,14; Mt. 10,1f.; Mk. 6,7; Lk. 9,1; 6,13; Mt. 10,5; 11,1; 19,28; 20,17; 26,14.20; Mk. 11,11; Lk. 8,1).

However this may be, the term "apostle," occurring as it does in Holy Scripture with extraordinary frequency, needs a more detailed explanation. It is probably not wrong to recognize in it a technical expression. The institution of the apostle, we may say, has its predecessor in the late-Judaic judicial institution of the *shaliach*. This has its roots far back in the Old Testament (cf. 2 Chron. 17,7-9), although its actual formation dates only from around the time of Jesus. The *shaliach* is the agent of an individual or group of persons.

The crucial thing here is authorization. The *shaliach* can be assigned any task. The fundamental legal principle applies: the emissary is as the man himself. However, he also has the duty to carry out his mission exactly, not in the sense of a mechanical execution of a command, but with a conscious decision for the plan and mission of another. Christ transformed the Jewish institution of the *sheluchim* for his purpose, filling it with religious content and moving it out of the merely legal sphere into the realm of revelation. The *sheluchim* called by Christ had only the one mission of representing him. The full power of authority which was his from the Father he transferred to the apostles, to use independently and responsibly, although without ceasing to be bound to him. Thus this word applies: "Whoever listens to you listens to me; whoever rejects you rejects me. And whoever rejects me rejects the One who sent me" (Lk. 10,16). The apostles are accordingly, through Jesus' own authorization, the empowered agents of the heavenly Father. Hence the rejection of the apostles means nothing less than the rejection of God himself (cf. Jn. 15,20).

The transformation of meaning undergone by this authorization of the apostles when Jesus recognized that his mission would be frustrated by the opposition of the Jews is expressed in his disclosure to the apostles of the mystery of his passion, very much to their surprise and horror. But it was especially revealed during their farewell meal, in the exclusive invitation to the founding assembly of the new People of God and in the commission to celebrate this memorial of his death. The calling took place before Easter, but later the risen Lord renewed their selection and sealed their commission. Only then were they finally constituted apostles. They received from Jesus the commission to be his witnesses, to testify to him as the Messiah and the glorified Lord. They participated in the appearances of the risen Lord, and for that reason they could be witnesses to the resurrection (Mt. 28,18-20; Acts 1,8).

At this point it becomes clear what constitutes an apostle. There are two elements: the encounter with the Risen One and the personal commission by him (Lk. 24,48; Acts 13,31; 2,32; 3,15; 4,20; 5,32; 10,39-43). These two main elements, however, imply a third. The appointed apostle must also have been with the Lord during his earthly life (Acts 1,21f.). By the experience of the

Risen One and of the historical life of Jesus is meant not only an acquaintance with the events as such but also the requisite spiritual understanding of the salvation-event (cf. 1 Jn. 1-4). Just as the first-hand participation in the earthly life of Jesus does not suffice for the constitution of an apostle without express authorization by Jesus, neither does the encounter with the Risen One of itself.

The calling and authorization by Jesus are indispensable. The spiritual understanding, however, is evoked by the sending of the Holy Spirit, which in turn supposes the commission by Christ. The role of apostle must be interpreted with reference not only to Christ but to the Spirit also.[2]

In this conception of "apostle" a serious difficulty arises as to whether, and in what sense, Paul can be considered an apostle. He had no association with Jesus during his earthly life. Even the event on the road to Damascus differs essentially from the appearances of the Risen One to the other apostles. Nevertheless Paul claims to be an apostle called not by men but by Jesus Christ and by God the Father who raised Jesus from the dead (Gal. 1,1f.). Paul defends his apostolic authorization with the greatest trenchancy and passion against Judaizing agitation which seeks to undermine his work (cf. Gal. 1,6ff.; also Rom. 1,1). He believes that he has been called directly by Jesus himself. Even though he did not know the historical Jesus, he nevertheless considers himself bound to the work and word of Jesus. He does not intend to proclaim a new gospel but the one given to him from the tradition of the earlier apostles. Despite his independence and freedom of interpretation, he regards the gospel of the earlier apostles as the binding norm for his own proclamation of Christ. Under the sway of the Holy Spirit he expounds the message of the earlier apostles in such a way that his own gospel is the explication of what was contained in the tradition (cf. Gal. 1,13-20; 2,2; Acts 9,26-30; 1 Cor. 11,23-29; 15,5). His gospel is,

[2]See A. Vögtle, "Zwölf," in *Lexicon für Theologie und Kirche*, X (1965²), 1443–1459; 4. "Paulus als Apostel." *Lexicon für Theologie und Kirche* is hereafter cited as *LTK*.

equally with that of the earlier apostles, the message about the crucified and resurrected Lord, the *kerygma* that Jesus is the Messiah, the Exalted One of God. The original apostles, then, also recognized Paul as an apostle, although they were not able to include him in the circle of the Twelve and although he had been baptized (Acts 9,18; 22,16), while nothing of that kind is reported of the other apostles. What sets Paul in opposition to the other apostles, especially in opposition to Peter in quite a marked way, is his negative opinion about the necessity for salvation of the Jewish rite of circumcision—that is, the idea that it is possible for man to please God by his own efforts and that he knows which efforts are necessary for this. Here we are, of course, dealing with a most fundamental question. On this matter, however, Paul is only expressing, boldly and decisively, what comprised the faith of the early apostles in the saving activity of Jesus Christ, and he even vindicates Peter before the others (Acts 15,6-21). Basically there was, at this point, only an either–or: either man partakes of salvation by his own efforts, or else he receives salvation as a gift of God. No one recognized this either–or with such clarity or pursued it with such decisiveness as Paul. In principle, however, there was no opposition in faith but only in the initial practice; this may be observed from the so-called Apostolic Council in Jerusalem, where Paul was assigned to the mission among the Gentiles, while Peter and the other apostles were to work among the Jews (Acts 15). Although this distinction was not strictly observed, the decision itself is of fundamental significance. The early apostles are apparently convinced that they are doing justice to the command of Jesus to carry the gospel to the ends of the earth by sending Paul to the Gentiles (Gal. 2,7; Acts 15). And Paul, in turn, showed his tie with Jerusalem in a special way when he zealously had a collection for the poor of that church taken up (Rom. 15,26-28; 1 Cor. 16,1-3; 2 Cor. 8,9ff.; Acts 24,17ff.; Gal. 2,10).

It should be mentioned that in Scripture the term "apostle" occasionally occurs also in a wider sense (cf. 1 Cor. 9,1.5f.; Rom. 16,7; Gal. 1,19f.; 1 Cor. 4,6.9; 1 Thess. 2,7). Apparently it soon lost its original meaning.

THE AUTHORITY OF THE APOSTLES

When his intention with regard to the appointment of the Twelve was changed as a result of his anticipated rejection by the Jews, Jesus interpreted more clearly, or rather enlarged, their authority for the new People to be founded. He says, "Whatever you bind on earth shall be bound in heaven, and whatever you loose on earth shall be loosed in heaven" (Mt. 18,18, *RSV*).[3] These words, taken from rabbinic language and probably addressed only to the Twelve, are meant to transmit a threefold authority to the apostles. First of all, they can declare something forbidden or permitted, but they can also impose an obligation or lift it, exclude from the Church or readmit into it, decree a ban or remove it. When the Twelve exercise disciplinary power in the house of God, they must be in a position to decide authoritatively what is right before God, that is, what is permitted and what is forbidden. Disciplinary authority has teaching power as its indispensable presupposition. Authoritative decisions can be enforced by penalties. The decision of the apostles is to have not only external legal force but internal spiritual force. It is to bind in the realm of conscience. What the apostles ordain is acknowledged by God as his own decision. Obedience or disobedience to the decrees of the apostles is in principle determinative of the eternal destiny of man (cf. Mt. 19,28).

A far-reaching interpretation of the power conferred upon the apostles, probably also a specific variation of the terms binding and loosing as used by Matthew, is given when Jesus is described after his resurrection as granting them the power to forgive sins. Because the passage is so important, it is quoted here (Jn. 20,19-23):

Late that Sunday evening, when the disciples were together behind locked doors, for fear of the Jews, Jesus came and stood among them.

---

[3] *RSV: Revised Standard Version and the Apocrypha*, copyrighted 1957 by the Division of Christian Education, National Council of the Churches of Christ in the U.S.A., and used by permission.

"Peace be with you!" he said, and then showed them his hands and his side. So when the disciples saw the Lord, they were filled with joy. Jesus repeated, "Peace be with you!" and then said, "As the Father sent me, so I send you." He then breathed on them, saying, "Receive the Holy Spirit! If you forgive any man's sins, they stand forgiven; if you pronounce them unforgiven, unforgiven they remain."

Through the forgiveness of sins in baptism and penance, man is received into the community of the believers in Christ or readmitted into it. He is made a partaker in that memorial meal which is to be celebrated until the end of time. The authorization to forgive sin presupposes the saving death on Calvary and the new life in the resurrection and in the Spirit. The apostles were to mediate to men the saving fruit of Calvary and of Easter morning.

The fullness of the apostolic authority promised by Jesus during his earthly life and confirmed after the resurrection culminated ultimately in the so-called great missionary command (and the other words of commission) of the Risen One to the disciples. In Mt. 28,16-20 we read:

The eleven disciples made their way to Galilee, to the mountain where Jesus had told them to meet him. When they saw him, they fell prostrate before him, though some were doubtful. Jesus then came up and spoke to them. He said: "Full authority in heaven and on earth has been committed to me. Go forth therefore and make all nations my disciples, baptize men everywhere in the name of the Father and of the Son and the Holy Spirit, and teach them to observe all that I have commanded you. And be assured, I am with you always, to the end of time." (Cf. Lk. 24,44-49; Mk. 16, 15-18.)

The formulation of this passage is derived from cultic sources; it is a later addition to the gospel, rather than the actual words of Jesus; but it apparently represents the tradition of the church in Jerusalem.

The statement has three parts: (1) the word of authorization, which constitutes the beginning and the basis for that which follows; (2) the command to instruct and baptize; (3) the promise. Although during his earthly ministry Jesus knew himself sent by the Father's commission only to Israel (cf. Mt. 10, 5f.; 15,24f.; Mk. 1,38), the commission with which the apostles are now entrusted applies to all of mankind. The situation has changed because of the death of Jesus. The final salvation achieved by his death and resurrection and the news of this are intended for all men (cf. Mk. 10,35; 13,10; 24,14). In this connection it should be remembered that the distinction of Jesus' disciples from the Jewish national community had already been prepared for during Jesus' life (cf. Mt. 3,7-10; Lk. 3,8; Jn. 8,33.37.39f.). The apostles are to convert all nations—that is, all of mankind—into believing disciples. Israel is not excluded, for the expression "all nations" does not mean just the Gentile nations as opposed to Jerusalem; it includes Israel. The missionary command includes the command to baptize. Man becomes a Christian by the believing acceptance of Jesus' message. This faith takes shape in baptism, which appears here as admission into the Body of Christ, to communion with Jesus and the disciples.

To prevent Christians from losing courage and despairing in the face of this mission to be fulfilled before heaven and earth—a mission decisive for the destiny of all men, for all of human history and for the cosmos—the promise is added that Jesus will remain with them until the end of time. Here it is clear again that the disciples commissioned by Jesus are considered his representatives (*sheluchim*). This implies that they carry out everything ordered, and nothing else. They can fulfill their task only in obedience to their Lord, but they themselves are responsible. Not only does obedience not preclude their own decision, but in fact this obedience demands such decision for Jesus, continually renewed. Thus the discharge of their entrusted task will at the same time have their human touch. The responsibility of the disciples appears more prominently in the synoptic gospels, whereas in the Johannine writings Jesus' part is more prominent. John puts more stress on the inner, personal relationship, the communality of life, between Christ and the faithful (Jn. 10, 1-16.27-29; 13,34f.; 17,6-26). We can say that the Johannine words of commission express more clearly the inner nature of that which the disciples are to do in the communion of life with Jesus, which means in the sacramental dimension.

THE COMMISSION TO PETER

The charge which was given to all the apostles received a special qualification and culmination in the authority bestowed upon Peter; the claim to inherit this has been the foundation of the papacy. In the gospels Peter appears from the beginning as the spokesman for the others (Mk. 8,29; Mt. 18,21; Lk. 9,5; 12,41; Jn. 6,67f.). In the synoptic lists of the apostles he is always named first (Mk. 3,16-19; Mt. 10,1-4; Lk. 6,12-16; Acts 1,13). His preeminence is also apparent in the expression "Peter and his companions" (Mk. 1,26; Lk. 9,32; Mk. 16,7). It is Peter who wants to bring Jesus back when he withdraws into solitude (Lk. 5,1-11f.; Mk. 1,36). It is Peter who asks Jesus about the reward of discipleship (Mk. 10,28), who wants to keep him from his death and has to be sharply rebuked for it (Mk. 8,32), who hastens on the waves to meet Jesus, walking on the sea (Mt. 14, 28-32). With James and John he belongs to Jesus' intimate circle (Mk. 5,37; 9,2f.; 14,33f.; cf. also Jn. 18,10; Mk. 14,47). The collectors of the temple tax turn first, as a matter of course, to Peter (Mt. 17,24f.). Peter is named first among those to whom Jesus appeared, although chronologically he was not first (1 Cor. 15,5). This last reference, which the apostle Paul received from tradition, is of great importance, as it expresses precisely this point, that Peter is the main witness to the resurrection of Jesus.

There are three primary references by which Peter's calling to a special position is attested: Mt. 16,13-19; Lk. 22,31f.; Jn. 21,15-17. According to the first, Simon answered the question of Jesus as to whom the disciples considered him to be with

"You are the Messiah, the Son of the living God." And Jesus answered him, "Simon, son of Jonah, you are favored indeed! You did not learn that from mortal man; it was revealed to you by my heavenly Father. And I say this to you: You are Peter, the Rock; and on this rock I will build my church, and the forces of death shall never overpower it. I will give you the keys of the kingdom of heaven; what you forbid on earth shall be forbidden in heaven, and what you allow on earth shall be allowed in heaven."

This narrative is inserted in Matthew before Jesus' prophecies of the passion. Mark and Luke report the scene of Jesus' question and Peter's answer, but not the promise of authority to Peter stated in Matthew (Mk. 8,27-30; Lk. 9,18-21).

Both the historical genuineness of the passage in Matthew and its meaning have been the subject of heated discussion in the history of exegesis up to our own day. Luther, Erasmus, and Calvin refer "the rock" to the invisible Church, which rests upon Christ or upon faith in him. In this opinion Peter is the rock insofar as he recognized Jesus in his messianic activity. Hence the Church is founded upon the faith which Peter experienced and confessed in that hour. The genuineness of the passage itself was not doubted until the last decades of the nineteenth century. After Harnack accepted it as belonging to the original gospel of Matthew and as originating in Jerusalem—because the text has a thoroughly Aramaic tone ("flesh and blood"; the term "Bar Jona"; the phrase about the "keys"; or the play on the words "rock" and "Peter"; as well as the expression "gates of hell" and the formula about "binding and loosing")—the genuineness of the passage was no longer questioned by the greater number of Protestant theologians. It is found in all ancient manuscripts and translations, and it is cited by Tertullian, Cyprian, and Origen.

We must realize that Jesus himself did not use the term *ecclesia*, or "church," as we find it in Matthew. However, that in no way rules out his having spoken about the building of a new community upon Peter. For that purpose, as we saw earlier, a number of formulations could be used. Even though the phrase "the church" must be explained form-critically—that is, by the history of tradition, or by redaction criticism—the factuality of the words of Jesus is not therefore compromised.

Why exactly Peter should receive such a special position is just as difficult to explain as the fact that a particular people, a certain woman, and a particular small community in Palestine were chosen by God for the incarnation of the eternal Logos.

As far as Peter's position in the early Church is concerned, there is a contradiction involved if one tries on the one hand to explain the Matthew passage as a creation of the early Church, and claims on the other hand that Peter never occupied the position which should have been his according to the passage in Matthew. Furthermore, the extent to which Peter enjoyed special recognition is clearly apparent from the behavior of Paul. Acts also illustrates Peter's special position in several ways, although it portrays Peter's activity against the background of the activity of the Twelve (Acts 8,4; 6,2ff.). But Peter is the one who matters most (Acts 8,14ff.). It is he who initiates the mission to the Gentiles, even though he manifests timidity and anxiety about doing so.

A separate question from that about the genuineness of the word of promise is the one as to whether the word was spoken in the framework described by Matthew or whether the insertion into the scene at the Sea of Galilee is to be explained as the work of an editor. In any case the word could only have been spoken at a time when Jesus had to recognize the fruitlessness of his efforts for the whole of the Israelite people. Because from that time on he began to prepare a new community, and the word to Peter is an important element in this process of preparation.

With regard to the content of the promise, let us first of all consider the changing of the name. A name is, according to ancient conceptions, not a mere label, but the expression of a character or a task; hence the giving of a name is a serious procedure. The assuming of a new name occurs in the course of salvation history only on the occasion of a decisive turning-point (cf. Gen. 2,19f.23; 3,20; 4,1; 5,29; 16,11; 17,5; 32,29; 41,45; 1 Sam. 1,20; 2 Kings 24,17; 2 Chron. 36,4; Num. 13,9-17; Is. 17,14; 8,3; 62,2; Hos. 2,16ff.; Dan. 1,7). When Jesus gave Simon the name, or rather the surname, Cephas, he was expressing his intention to give him a new responsibility, a new position. The name Simon was not replaced by the name Cephas; the latter was only added. Jesus himself continued to address Simon by his original name till the end (Mt. 17,25; Mk. 14,37; Lk. 22,31.34; Jn. 21,15-17). The evangelists usually call him Simon Peter (Lk. 5,8; Jn. 1,41; 6,8.68, etc.), or simply Peter. In the early Church the apostle Peter is called first of all by the Aramaic form *Kepha*, then by the Greek form *Cephas*. Paul almost always calls him Cephas (Gal. 1,18;

2,7ff.11.14; 1 Cor. 1,12; 3,22; 9,5; 15,5; cf. Gal. 2,7.8). For him apparently the term has already become a proper name deriving from the fact that it designates Peter's function.

According to the word of Jesus, Peter is to be the rock, the foundation of the Church. In this promise Christ employs the image of a building (cf. Jn. 2,19; Mk. 14,58; 15,29). In order that the building erected by him may have durability and stability, its foundation must be a rock. But this foundation as contemplated by Jesus is to be a person. The question arises, Which function in the personal realm is capable of giving a community unshakable stability, support and security, unity and permanence? It can only be the leadership of the Church. Since the Church is the recipient of such initial leadership, it will be protected from the threatening dangers of the gates of hell—i.e., from transitoriness. "Gates of hell" does not mean the power of evil, or unbelief, or immorality, or hate, or the devil, but the force of transitoriness. When Paul names Christ himself as the foundation to be built upon, he indicates that everyone empowered by Christ must proclaim not himself but Christ. Peter represents that rock foundation which is Jesus himself. In Peter it makes its appearance; it is active. Peter is the medium of that function which Paul means when he speaks of Christ as the rock.

According to the Epistle to the Ephesians (2,19f.), the other apostles also, together with the prophets and other charismatics, are the foundation upon which the house of God is built.

What is thus portrayed by the image of the rock is developed by two other figures, the image of the keys of the kingdom of heaven and the metaphor of binding and loosing. The keys are a symbol showing that Peter represents upon earth the Lord and owner of the house, namely Christ. With the transfer of the keys, according to rabbinic linguistic usage, he is installed as the deputy of Christ. In the household of the community of Christ, of the new People of God, the highest regulatory power belongs to Peter as vicar of the Lord of the house. This power also includes the authority to teach. The rabbis exercise the power of the keys by proclaiming the will of God set forth in the Torah through preaching, teaching and judging, and thus they open to the community the access to the reign of God (according to the teaching of Jesus, of course, they close it off: Mt. 23,13). Christ, as the only one with such authority, using the words of an established formula, promises Simon the power of dispensing the saving benefits of the reign of God (A. Vögtle). By the word of his proclamation, he opens the way to Christ, which means to God, to the Father in heaven. The steward of the house and the bearer of the keys has to decide what is right according to God's order, what is to be permitted and what forbidden. Thus the image of the keys is a transition into the image of the power to bind and loose.

On the other hand, what Jesus bestows on Peter with this word of binding and loosing he grants to all the apostles, according to Mt. 18,18.

In the sayings of Jesus the expressions "church" and "kingdom of heaven" are used without any clear distinction. The power of the keys refers to the "kingdom of heaven." Peter, in the text from Matthew, is the rock upon which the Church is founded. The kingdom of heaven and the Church are not identical, but they stand in close connection insofar as the Church is the beginning and at the same time the instrument for bringing about the kingdom of God. Peter and the apostles open the way to the kingdom of God by giving access to the Church, by means of proclamation and guidance.

Another passage which concerns Peter is Lk. 22,29-32. There arose among the disciples a quarrel about which of them was the greatest. In his answer Jesus says, among other things: "I vest in you the kingship which my Father vested in me; you shall eat and drink at my table in my kingdom and sit on thrones as judges of the twelve tribes of Israel. 'Simon, Simon, take heed: Satan has been given leave to sift all of you like wheat; but for you I have prayed that your faith may not fail; and when you have come to yourself, you must lend strength to your brothers.'" It is as surprising as it is significant that Christ speaks first of all of Satan's assault upon all the disciples, but then declares that he is praying for Peter. Satan will use the passion of Jesus as a temptation to shake the faith of the disciples. The prayer of Jesus is that the faith of Peter shall not give way. It is evident that the steadfastness of this man or his fall will be decisive for all.

Peter appears also to suffer a special crisis of faith. As the promises given to him are especially great, so he seems to be exposed to particularly difficult temptations. In the denial which Jesus predicts in vv. 33 and 34 of the above passage, Peter in fact succumbs to the temptation. The prayer of Jesus, however, kept Peter from losing his faith completely. This was important because the apostle was to give support to his brethren, i.e., the Church. So Jesus prayed for Peter in view of the future Church. As soon as Peter himself has again achieved a complete faith, he is also to strengthen the others. Such a statement was not addressed to anyone else.

According to the testimony of the gospel of John, Jesus fulfills his promises to Peter after the resurrection. It is understandable that the confirmation of his position should take place after the resurrection, for the life of the Church is bound to the resurrection of the Lord. His historical existence was prelude and preparation. What John (21,15-19) reports appears as a fulfillment of that which was promised in Matthew and Luke. This is the passage in which Jesus summons Peter to feed his lambs and his sheep.

The question put to Peter three times, "Peter, do you love me?" is not to be construed as a reminder of Peter's denial. It was a rite of installation or transfer of authority customary in that time. In solemn juridical manner the risen Christ entrusts to Peter the care of his flock. This image of the flock and of the shepherd played an important role in the Old as well as in the New Testament. Christ describes himself as the Good Shepherd (Jn. 10) who cares for his sheep (Mt. 18,12-14; Lk. 15,4-6). The flock is small (Lk. 12,32), but it need not be afraid, for it has pleased the Father to give the kingdom to it (Mt. 10,16). The shepherd, according to the Old Testament, is to search for pastures and watering places for his flock (Ps. 23,2f.; Gen. 31,4; Ex. 2,16). It is also his responsibility to protect the flock from attacks and dangers (1 Sam. 17,34f.; Jn. 10,12) and to maintain order within it, so that the stronger animals will not keep the weaker ones away from the best pastures. The Shepherd's staff is used for carrying out these tasks (1 Sam. 17,40.50). Christ himself let his role as shepherd cost him his life (Jn. 10,11; 10,16; cf. Ez. 34). Then Christ added, as he announced to Peter his own martyrdom, "Follow me."

The special position of the apostle Peter is confirmed by Acts and especially by Paul. In Acts, Peter is described as the spiritual leader of the young Church, conscious of his responsibility; as the successful and courageous preacher of the gospel; as the guardian, possessing disciplinary powers against unholy conditions within the Church; and finally, as the pace-setter for the missionary activity, breaching the barriers of Judaism (cf. Acts 1,15-26; 2,14-40; 4,8; 5,29; 5,1-11; 3,1-26; 8,14-17; 8,18-25; 9,32-43).

The most important single act of the apostle was his baptizing of the Gentile centurion Cornelius and his whole household in Caesarea (Acts 10). With this action Peter crossed the boundaries of his own people and carried the witness of Christ to the Gentiles. This act retains its significance even though for a long time there continued to be hesitation both on the part of Peter himself and of the whole community of Jerusalem with regard to the role of the Jewish ritual law of circumcision (cf. Acts 11,1-18; 12,1-19). Peter played a decisive role at the Apostolic Council in the year 49-50 (Acts 15). By his speech in favor of freedom from the Jewish ritual law, against Judaizing efforts, he brought about the decision not to impose upon the Gentile Christians the burden of circumcision, although in the interest of peace and as a concession to the traditional believers some prescriptions were still imposed upon the citizens of Antioch. In the opinion of Paul, Peter was evidently the most important personality in Jerusalem (Gal. 1,18; 1 Cor. 15,3; Acts 9,26).

The argument in Antioch, reported in the letter to the Galatians, plays no small role in helping us to evaluate the relationship between Paul and Peter. Here Paul states (Gal. 2,11-21) that he opposed Peter face to face because Peter was in the wrong. It seems that some Christians had come from Jerusalem and criticized Peter for his fellowship with the Gentile Christians. After the arrival of these people from Jerusalem, Peter fearfully withdrew. Even Barnabas, Paul's companion, gave in. Thus the unity of the Christian community in Antioch was disturbed, and at the same time the freedom of Christianity from the Jewish ritual law was threatened. Disappointed and shocked, Paul saw his work endangered. With characteristic decisiveness he re-

buked Peter for his "hypocrisy." He reproached him for jeop-
ardizing the unity and the truth of the gospel against his own
conviction, and doing this simply out of fear of men. Obviously
the question in Antioch is not one of doctrinal difference between
Paul and Peter, but of inconsistent conduct. Paul did not direct his
rebuke to Barnabas but to Peter, because Peter's example was
decisive.

It should be pointed out that the passage in Mt. 16,16-19, which
according to the form critics is a genuine saying of the Lord,
originating in Palestine, could be accepted into the gospel only by
a generation in which that which the passage claims was a fact.
Therefore, Peter must necessarily have been known as the
leading man in the Church at the time when the gospel of
Matthew was beginning to circulate. The Church would have
made itself ridiculous by having the gospel circulating at a time
when many people remembered Peter, if he had not functioned in
the way it describes.

THE SENDING OF THE SPIRIT

The activity of Jesus in founding the Church was completed only
with the sending of the Spirit. The Church exists only from the
day of Pentecost. It can be seen completely only when it is
viewed from the aspect both of Christ and of the Spirit. The
statement that the Church was founded at Pentecost has to be
understood in this way, that Jesus decided and prepared the
essential elements, but in its concrete realization it is primarily
the accomplishment of the Holy Spirit, resulting, in the last
analysis, from Israel's refusal to believe (cf. Rom. 9ff.).[4] When
Jesus, according to Acts (1,4-6), commanded his followers not to
leave Jerusalem but to await the promise of the Father, we
understand that the power of the Holy Spirit was to come over
them. This sending of the Spirit took place publicly, just as the
crucifixion of Christ took place before the gates of the city in
public view.

The signs of the descended Spirit cannot be overlooked or

[4]J. Ratzinger, "Kirche," in *LTK*, VI (1961), 177.

ignored. Fire as a symbol of God's coming was not unknown to those who experienced at first hand the events of that morning (Exod. 3,2; 14,20.28; 19,18; 24,17; Heb. 12,29). Fire is a symbol both of the grace of God and of his anger. Whoever refuses the self-communication of God will receive it at judgment (Jn. 14,16f.; 15,26 to 16,15). The self-communication of God in the sending of the Spirit produced misunderstanding and scandal, even as the incarnation of the Logos had. Mixed with the wonder of some was the ridicule of others (Acts 2,13; cf. Eph. 5,18). In the power of the Spirit, Peter, in the name of all the others, bore witness before the assembled crowds to Jesus, whom the Jews had killed but who the Father had awakened to life and so solemnly testified to as his Messiah, and who now sits at the right hand of God as had been foretold of the messianic time. Everyone can share in this Spirit if he will do penance and be baptized in the name of Jesus Christ (Acts 2,14–38).

The Spirit sent by Jesus from the Father does not act like an automatic force, but rather moves men to their own decision. Thus the concrete shaping of the Church from that Pentecost day on has been decided not only by the will of Jesus Christ but also by the decision of the men called by him. Peter's preaching was the result of the gift of the Spirit, but it corresponded also to his personal style of thought and speech. Ever since that day, the Church reveals itself as a combination of the work of God and man, a divine-human reality. It would be a misinterpretation of the gospel to identify the Spirit with the community. It would likewise contradict Scripture to exclude from the constitution of the Church the spontaneity and the historical character of human activity. There remains in the action of the Spirit human freedom with all its nuances.

What the Holy Spirit gave to the disciples was a true understanding of Jesus Christ and his work, which till then they had not rightly comprehended. Shortly before the ascension it was evident that they still had not understood Jesus and his mission, either in its spiritual or in its eschatological character (Acts 1,6; cf. Mk. 4,13–40; 6,50–52; 7,18; 8,16–21; 9,9f.32; 14,37–41; Lk. 18,34; Jn. 2,22; 12,16; 13,7.28f.; 14,5.8f.; 16,12; 17f.). The Spirit revealed to them the mystery of Jesus and of the kingdom of God.

Now they recognize Jesus Christ in the light of Scripture as the Messiah confirmed by God himself (Lk. 24,25–37; Jn. 2,22; 12,16; 12,9; Acts 2,25–35; 3,13.22–25; 4,11.24–28; 10,43; 1 Cor. 15,3). The preaching described in the Acts of the Apostles is an example of this. The Spirit also produces in the apostles a fearlessness in the face of danger and torture, so that nothing can induce them to give up their witnessing to Christ. With candor and confidence, with joyousness and steadfastness, before the high council and the whole nation, they proclaim Jesus as the Lord, as the Messiah sent from the God of the Old Testament. The Spirit also reveals to the hearers the meaning of the witness of the apostles, so that they understand, are converted, and are baptized (Acts 2,41). An effect of the presence of the Spirit in the young Church was the flourishing life which is described in Acts 2,42–47. The members of the fledgling Church, on the basis of the apostolic proclamation, united in a holy fear of God over all the many wonders, were so much one heart and one soul that they joyfully and lovingly shared their goods with the needy. The love which moved them in the power of the Spirit was so great that it could later be said that the Church was built upon a foundation of apostles and prophets (Eph. 2,20).

According to this explanation the Church is an effect from above, not from below, an act of God rather than a voluntary association of men in response to a religious need. On the other hand, it must be emphasized (cf. *Mystici Corporis*) that without the free decision of those called by God, membership in the Church would never come to pass. In this sense the Church is the voluntary association of its members, insofar as these by a free decision take on membership through faith and baptism. However, when a man has once become a member of the Church, he remains that forever. For in baptism he receives an ineradicable mark (sacramental character).

◄ 5

The Glorified Christ and the Spirit (as Lasting Foundation of the Church)

THE HUMAN AND THE DIVINE IN THE CHURCH

If in the preceding exposition Christ and the Holy Spirit have been called the source of the Church, the statement is intended first of all to refer to the activity of a particular time, namely the time between the incarnation and the sending of the Spirit. But the word "source" goes beyond this sense. For the glorified Lord and the Holy Spirit sent by him, or rather the glorified Lord in the Holy Spirit, remains forever present in the Church as the source of life, as Head, as Lord. The Church is marked until the end of time, until its final realization in the kingdom of God, by the saving presence of its heavenly Lord in the Holy Spirit.

But it also receives the unique impress of the men who constitute the Church. This unique quality is determined in the progress of history by the changes in men's attitude toward life, in modes of thought, in human desires and strivings, but also by the diversity of the various nations and peoples, with their diverse political, social, economic, and cultural forms and styles. So, despite the one faith in the Lord present in the Holy Spirit and despite the essential form of the Church determined by Christ, there remains nevertheless a great diversity, a diversity which can never be reduced to uniformity. Unity does not mean uniformity. For this reason we can speak of the Church in Europe or the Church in India or the ancient Church or the modern Church or today's Church. On account of its diversity the Church can remain truly living and vital. Were the diversity to disappear, then the Church would have the "order" of a cemetery.

The diversity leads naturally to tensions. We will see, however, that tension does not result in division as long as unity remains safeguarded in the communal celebration of the Eucharist. The Second Vatican Council expressed this fact as follows (Constitution on the Church, #8):

Christ, the one Mediator, established and ceaselessly sustains here on earth His holy Church, the community of faith, hope, and charity, as a visible structure. Through her He communicates truth and grace to all. But the society furnished with hierarchical agencies and the Mystical Body of Christ are not to be considered as two realities, nor are the visible assembly and the spiritual community, nor the earthly Church and the Church enriched with heavenly things. Rather they form one interlocked reality which is comprised of a divine and a human element. For this reason, by an excellent analogy, this reality is compared to the mystery of the incarnate Word. Just as the assumed nature inseparably united to the divine Word serves Him as a living instrument of salvation, so, in a similar way, does the communal structure of the Church serve Christ's Spirit, who vivifies it by way of building up the body (cf. Eph. 4,16).[1]

THE PRESENCE OF CHRIST IN THE CHURCH

There are three images which the Church applies to herself, by means of which she states her faith in the connection of the divine with the human, in the presence of the heavenly Lord in the visible society of believers: namely, the image of the People of God, that of the Body of Christ, and that of the Bride of Christ.

---

[1] *The Documents of Vatican II*, ed. Walter M. Abbott, S.J. (New York: America Press, 1966, 22. Excerpts from the Constitutions and Decrees of the Ecumenical Council are taken from *The Documents of Vatican II*, published by Guild Press, America Press, Association Press, and Herder and Herder, and copyrighted 1966 by the America Press. Used by permission.

There are certain connections between the three, so that they really say the same thing under different aspects. Common to all is the conviction of the vital relationship of the society of believers in Christ to the heavenly Lord present in the Holy Spirit and to his Father.

The Church as the People of God

As has already been emphasized, what is signified by the image of the Church as the People of God became, in the Second Vatican Council, the dominant concept in the self-understanding of the Church. We do not get an adequate understanding of this concept by first inquiring into the general meaning of a people or nation, and then looking for the specific difference between other peoples and the Church as the People of God. We must instead try (although against the background of the general idea of a people) to interpret the meaning of the Church as the People of God out of its own particular usage. To begin with an analysis of the idea of nation could lead to a misinterpretation, for we would immediately have to eliminate all those elements characteristic of a nation in the natural sense. It is a question, rather, of a society willed and created by God for his service. The specific difference is not between this people and other peoples, but between the Old Testament and New Testament peoples.

The Church is called the New Testament People of God in distinction to the Old Testament People of God; it is also called Body of Christ or Bride of Christ. Basically these two latter images convey the same idea as that of the People of God. It is a question of complementary ideas. A possible misunderstanding must be guarded against in advance, a misunderstanding which has frequently emerged in the course of history and the full development of the Church's life and often led to mutual recrimination—to the reproach of clericalism on the one hand and lay domination on the other. The phrase "People of God" does not designate a particular group of the faithful within the Church, as opposed to another group, the hierarchy. The concept refers to the whole Church, as a unity. The idea of a people does point to a boundary; not, however, to a line drawn within the Church, but to a line which marks the limit of the whole people. It separates those who are members from those who are not members of the People of God. Here we must nonetheless point out that there is no sharp division between that society which we call the People of God, or the People of Jesus Christ, and those men who do not nominally belong to this People. In some way all men are united with the Church as the People of God—many even in a very vital and interior relationship. It would be an unfortunate misunderstanding to think of the boundaries of the Church cutting off all other peoples separated from it by historical circumstances. Such a drawing of borders was possible and necessary in the Old Testament, where the People of God was limited to the successors of Abraham. The New Testament People of God, however, does not stand in opposition to the "Nations"—the "Gentiles"—but excludes only those who have no saving relation to Christ.

Since the connection between the Old Testament People of God and the Church has already been explained, as well as the radical difference between them, it will be necessary here only to recall briefly the witness of the New Testament to the Church as the heir to the Old Testament People of God. The Church refers to itself in the New Testament as the true Israel. The old Israel was a foreshadowing, a type of Israel in the spirit. This self-understanding is apparent, as we saw, in the word *ekklesia,* and occasionally we meet it also in the term "people" or "nation." The use of the term, however, is not the decisive thing. The reality itself pervades the entire New Testament, especially the Pauline letters. We find the concept of the Church as the spiritual People of God most prominent in the letter to the Galatians and in First Corinthians, where it stands at the center of Paul's ecclesiology, but it plays a decisive role also in the letter to the Romans. The pastoral letters, too, are filled with this belief. In the letter to the Colossians it is less prominent (cf. Gal. 3 and 4; 1 Cor.10,18; but also 2 Cor. 6,16; Rom. 4,1–25; most important, Rom. 9,11; and further, Phil. 3,2–4). Because the Christians are truly and really the children of Abraham, the sacred writings of the Old Testament belong to them, according to Paul. They were written for the spiritual Israel. The old Israel cannot understand its own Scriptures and its history (Rom. 15,4; 1 Cor. 9,10; 10,11; 2 Cor. 3,14ff.;

Tit. 82,13f.; see also Heb. 4,9; 8,10–13). There is a veil over its eyes.

The rest of the New Testament reinforces the idea of the Church as People of God (cf. Mt. 3,9; 8,11; 22,8f.; 23,38f.; Mk. 12,9ff.; Lk. 14,21ff.; Mt. 11,16–24; Mk. 13,2; Lk. 13,6f.; 19,41ff.; Mt. 5,13ff.; Lk. 12,32). The men who were the fathers of the former People are also the fathers of the new, according to the word of Jesus. For this reason they are the first invited into the new Church (Mt. 8,12; 21,43; Lk. 14,15ff.; Mt. 22,1ff.).

In the Acts of the Apostles the idea that the original community is the new People of God is fundamental. It appears clearly in the sermons of Peter and Paul mentioned above. Even though these are stylized, there appears in the composition a basic formula of the tradition. The first letter of Peter offers a particularly clear and rich witness (1 Pet. 2,4–11):

So come to him, our living Stone—the stone rejected by men but choice and precious in the sight of God. Come, and let yourselves be built, as living stones, into a spiritual temple; become a holy priesthood, to offer spiritual sacrifices acceptable to God through Jesus Christ. For it stands written: "I lay in Zion a choice cornerstone of great worth, the man who has faith in it will not be put to shame" (Is. 28,16). The great worth of which it speaks is for you who have faith. For those who have not faith, the stone which the builders rejected has become not only the cornerstone, but also "a stone to trip over, a rock to stumble against" (Ps. 118,22). They stumble when they disbelieve the Word. Such was their appointed lot! But you are a chosen race, a royal priesthood, a dedicated nation, and a people claimed by God for his own, to proclaim the triumphs of him who has called you out of darkness into his marvelous light. You are now the people of God, who once were not his people; outside his mercy once, you have now received his mercy.

The Church is similarly characterized in the apocalypse of John (cf. Rev. 18; 21,3f.). Jesus is the Lord of this People.

In post-apostolic times the idea of the People of God is taken up, although it is not expanded (cf., e.g., the *Shepherd of Hermas*, 2,2.6, or Justin Martyr, *Dial.*, 123,6f.9; or Irenaeus, *Against the False Gnosis*, 4,36; 4,2; 4,15,2; 3,9,1). Hippolytus is particularly explicit about it. Origen sees in the Church the true Israel. In the

Latin Church this concept of the Church as People of God was carried on by Cyprian and Tertullian, and especially by Augustine. Tertullian defends the unity of the Old Testament and New Testament People of God against Gnosticism (*Against Marcion*, 1,21; *Apology*, 21,4). It must be noted, however, that with Tertullian the use of this image of the People of God applied to the Church begins to decline. The Church is the People of God only as the Spirit-filled society of believers in Christ. It is no longer those who are of different race and blood who are the outsiders, but those who do not share in the new birth by which men become members of this People. The use of the concept of People of God is misapplied by Tertullian to mean essentially the eucharistic community. Cyprian has a twofold concept of the People. The first is derived from the order of the community in the liturgy, and it refers to the laity who are united with the bishop and take part in the eucharistic celebration only as receivers. The second is taken from Scripture and refers to the Church as the spiritual nation of believers, which has taken the place of God's former People. This second concept is closely related to the eucharistic celebration, for the People in this second sense present themselves at the Eucharist. Cyprian's first concept gradually began to prevail, as the idea of the People came more and more to have the meaning "community of the laity." This concept became superimposed on the still prevalent older one which had arisen out of the Old and New Testaments.

In Augustine also we find the two ideas. He stresses that the People of God is characterized by its relation to Christ, being in fact the Body of Christ. In the time after Augustine the more limited concept gradually prevailed, although the more comprehensive one was never entirely forgotten. It is retained above all in the liturgy of the Church, especially in the texts of the Mass, although here also the later, particular concept is not absent (e.g., the prayer after the consecration: "We, your servants, as also your holy people"). Related to the idea of People of God is the image of the Church as a family, a concept which we meet frequently in the liturgy.

The Second Vatican Council treats this idea of the Church as People of God in a separate chapter, II of the Constitution on the

Church *(Lumen Gentium)*. Here it refers to the fundamental connection between the Old and the New Testament Peoples of God, and it cites the passage from 1 Peter 2 quoted above. At the same time, the Council strongly emphasizes the quality given to this People by the presence of Christ in the Spirit. It becomes evident that the idea is not a general idea that can be applied to all nations, but one which takes on a specific meaning when used of the Church as People of God. The application of the concept requires special attention to the analogy which is present in all theological statements. There are several texts in the Constitution on the Church which are particularly relevant:

(#9). That messianic people has for its head Christ, "who was delivered up for our sins, and rose again for our justification" (Rom. 4,25), and who now, having won a name which is above all names, reigns in glory in heaven. The heritage of this people are the dignity and freedom of the sons of God, in whose hearts the Holy Spirit dwells as in His temple. Its law is the new commandment to love as Christ loved us (cf. Jn. 13,34). Its goal is the kingdom of God, which has been begun by God himself on earth, and which is to be further extended until it is brought to perfection by Him at the end of time. Then Christ our life (cf. Col. 3,4) will appear, and "creation itself also will be delivered from its slavery to corruption into the freedom of the glory of the sons of God" (Rom. 8,21).

So it is that this messianic people, although it does not actually include all men, and may more than once look like a small flock, is nonetheless a lasting and sure seed of unity, hope, and salvation for the whole human race. Established by Christ as a fellowship of life, charity, and truth, it is also used by Him as an instrument for the redemption of all, and is sent forth into the whole world as the light of the world and the salt of the earth (cf. Mt. 5,13–16).

(#13). All men are called to belong to the new People of God. Wherefore this People, while remaining one and unique, is to be spread throughout the whole world and must exist in all ages, so that the purpose of God's will may be fulfilled. In the beginning God made human nature one. After His children were scattered, He decreed that they should at length be unified again (cf. Jn. 11,52). It was for this reason that God sent His Son, whom He appointed heir of all things (cf. Heb. 1,2), that He might be Teacher, King and Priest of all, the Head of the new and universal people of the sons of God. For this God finally sent His Son's Spirit as Lord and

Lifegiver. He it is who, on behalf of the whole Church and each and every one of those who believe, is the principle of their coming together and remaining together in the teaching of the apostles and in fellowship, in the breaking of bread and in prayers (cf. Acts 2,42, Greek text).

For a clearer explanation of the question as to who belongs to the Church and how the boundary line is drawn between baptized and unbaptized, it will be useful to quote sections 14–16 in their entirety:

(#14). This sacred Synod turns its attention first to the Catholic faithful. Basing itself upon sacred Scripture and tradition, it teaches that the Church, now sojourning on earth as an exile, is necessary for salvation. For Christ, made present to us in His Body, which is the Church, is the one Mediator and the unique Way of salvation. In explicit terms He Himself affirmed the necessity of faith and baptism (cf. Mk. 16,16; Jn. 3,5) and thereby affirmed also the necessity of the Church, for through baptism as through a door men enter the Church. Whosoever, therefore, knowing that the Catholic Church was made necessary by God through Jesus Christ, would refuse to enter her or to remain in her could not be saved.

They are fully incorporated into the society of the Church, who, possessing the Spirit of Christ, accept her entire system and all the means of salvation given to her, and through union with her visible structure are joined to Christ, who rules her through the Supreme Pontiff and the bishops. This joining is effected by the bonds of professed faith, of the sacraments, of ecclesiastical government, and of communion. He is not saved, however, who though he is part of the body of the Church, does not persevere in charity. He remains indeed in the bosom of the Church, but, as it were, only in a "bodily" manner and not "in his heart." All the sons of the Church should remember that their exalted status is to be attributed not to their own merits but to the special grace of Christ. If they fail moreover to respond to that grace in thought, word, and deed, not only will they not be saved but they will be the more severely judged.

(#15). The Church recognizes that in many ways she is linked with those who, being baptized, are honored with the name of Christian, though they do not profess the faith in its entirety; or do not preserve unity of communion with the successor of Peter. For there are many who honor sacred Scripture, taking it as a norm of belief and of action, and who show a true religious zeal. They lovingly believe in God the Father

Almighty and in Christ, Son of God and Savior. They are consecrated by baptism, through which they are united with Christ. They also recognize and receive other sacraments within their own Churches or ecclesial communities. Many of them rejoice in the episcopate, celebrate the Holy Eucharist, and cultivate devotion toward the Virgin Mother of God. They also share with us in prayer and other spiritual benefits.

Likewise, we can say that in some real way they are joined with us in the Holy Spirit, for to them also He gives His gifts and graces, and is thereby operative among them with His sanctifying power. Some indeed he has strengthened to the extent of the shedding of their blood. In all of Christ's disciples the Spirit arouses the desire to be peacefully united, in the manner determined by Christ, as one flock under one shepherd, and He prompts them to pursue this goal. Mother Church never ceases to pray, hope, and work that they may gain this blessing. She exhorts her sons to purify and renew themselves so that the sign of Christ may shine more brightly over the face of the Church.

(#16). Finally, those who have not yet received the gospel are related in various ways to the People of God. In the first place there is the people to whom the covenants and the promises were given and from whom Christ was born according to the flesh (cf. Rom. 9,4–5). On account of their fathers, this people remains most dear to God, for God does not repent of the gifts He makes nor of the calls he issues (cf. Rom. 11,28–29).

But the plan of salvation also includes those who acknowledge the Creator. In the first place among these there are the Moslems, who, professing to hold the faith of Abraham, along with us adore the one and merciful God, who on the last day will judge mankind. Nor is God Himself far distant from those who in shadows and images seek the unknown God, for it is He who gives to all men life and breath and every other gift (cf. Acts 17,25–28), and who as Savior wills that all men be saved (cf. 1 Tim. 2,4).

Those also can attain to everlasting salvation who through no fault of their own do not know the gospel of Christ or His Church, yet sincerely seek God and, moved by grace, strive by their deeds to do His will as it is known to them through the dictates of conscience. Nor does divine Providence deny the help necessary for salvation to those who, without blame on their part, have not yet arrived at an explicit knowledge of God, but who strive to live a good life, thanks to His grace. Whatever goodness or truth is found among them is looked upon by the Church as a preparation for the gospel. She regards such qualities as given by Him who enlightens all men so that they may finally have life.

But rather often men, deceived by the Evil One, have become caught up in futile reasoning and have exchanged the truth of God for a lie, serving the creature rather than the Creator (cf. Rom. 1,21.25). Or some there are who, living and dying in a world without God, are subject to utter hopelessness. Consequently, to promote the glory of God and procure the salvation of all such men, and mindful of the command of the Lord, "Preach the gospel to every creature" (Mk. 16,16), the Church painstakingly fosters her missionary work.

Despite the uncertainty about the boundary, it is rightly emphasized by the Council that there is only one New Testament People of God, just as there was only one Old Testament People. In section 8 of the Constitution (ch. I) it is explained that the Church of Christ is unique, a Church which we confess as one, holy, catholic, and apostolic. After his resurrection our Savior commissioned Peter to tend this flock (Jn. 21,15ff.). He entrusted to him and to the other apostles the expansion and the leadership of the People of God (Mt. 28,18ff.), and he established the Church for all time as the pillar and bulwark of truth (1 Tim. 3,15). The awareness of the uniqueness of the Church, together with the impossibility of stating definitively who does not belong to it, or does not belong in full explicitness, is expressed in the Sentence: "This Church, constituted and organized in the world as a society, subsists in the Catholic Church, which is governed by the successor of Peter and by the bishops in union with that successor. . . . " (#8, Constitution on the Church). Here the visible structure of the Church is cited by the Council as an element of its self-understanding, but it adds immediately that this concrete existential form of the People of God in the Catholic Church is not exclusive, that "many elements of sanctification and of truth can be found outside of her visible structure. These elements, however, as gifts properly belonging to the Church of Christ, possess an inner dynamism toward Catholic unity" (#8).

The Church as the Body of Christ

The concept of the Church as the People of God is entirely compatible with the image of the Church as the Body of Christ, which is found only in the Pauline letters (although cf. Acts 9,4).

As the concept of People is completed by the image of Body of Christ, insofar as the latter shows the interiority of the bond between Christ and the faithful, so, on the other hand, the image of the People of God is a necessary complement to that of the Body of Christ, in order to show clearly the difference between Christ and the Church as the society of the believing faithful, so that the Church is not absorbed in a mystical identity with the existence of Christ but is seen as a dynamic society, truly imprinted with the mark of Christ, but in movement toward the Father, the first divine Person, to whom Christ is the way.

An explicit presentation of the Church as Body of Christ is given by Pius XII in the encyclical on the Mystical Body of Christ (cf. also his encyclical *Mediator Dei* of August 12, 1950). The Second Vatican Council devotes section 7 in its first chapter of the dogmatic Constitution on the Church to this subject. In the theology of the Fathers of the Church it was Augustine above all who developed this idea of Body of Christ. It is occasionally found in other theological and ecclesiastical documents, but it does not play a decisive role there.

In the Pauline epistles the idea appears very frequently, not always in exactly the same sense, but with different shades of meaning. Speaking quite generally, one can say that it contains the idea of the priority of the universal Church over the local church. The apostle did not find the concept of church as an organism in the Old Testament or within the apostolic tradition. It is his own creation, from which he constantly receives new stimuli for reflection. There is a difference between the use of the concept in the major epistles and that in the pastoral epistles. Nowhere in Paul do we meet the expression "mystical body of Christ"; this was a phrase added by a later theology. For a long time its meaning alternated, the Eucharist often being called the mystical body and the Church the true body, formed by the eucharistic body. After much unclearness of terminology, however, the word "mystical" applied to the Church in connection with the word "body" attained definite acceptance in the second half of the twelfth century and spread, until by the end of that century it had become common usage.

Paul speaks simply of the members of Christ or of the body of

Christ or of one body in Christ. We find his theme of the Church as the Body of Christ in 1 Corinthians, in Romans, and also in Ephesians and Colossians, but only in the two latter is it fully developed. The occasion for the interpretation of the Church as a body or as the body of Christ arose out of the different situations in the communities to which he was writing. In the sixth chapter of the First Epistle to the Corinthians it is a wrong conception of Christian freedom which moves the apostle to explain to the Corinthians that Christians are members of Christ and cannot dispose of themselves according to their own pleasure. As a result of baptism, the whole man in his bodily existence is the property of the Lord and therefore cannot do whatever he pleases. So close is the union which the Holy Spirit establishes between Christ and the Christian that the Christian belongs most intimately to Christ; he stands under the dominion of Jesus Christ and owes him obedience.

Paul develops the concept of the Body of Christ more explicitly and completely in the tenth chapter of the same letter (1 Cor. 10,14–17). The occasion is the participation of some of the Corinthians in the Gentiles' sacrificial meals. The Christians, because of their baptism, are living in communion with Christ. This is in irreconcilable conflict with the communion with the demons which is cultivated by participation in the Gentile sacrifices. According to Paul, the communion with Christ is founded in the fact that the cup of blessing establishes a union in the blood of Christ and that the bread broken in the communal meal establishes a union with the body of Christ, that is, with the whole Christ. Because the bread is one, he says, we all, though many, are one body. The sacramental body, or the eucharistic body of Jesus Christ, and the Church belong together as the (mystical) body of Jesus Christ. The eucharistic body is called by Paul the basis and the means of the body which is the Church.

Paul develops his doctrine of the Church as the Body of Christ most extensively in the twelfth chapter of the First Epistle to the Corinthians. He begins from a liturgical, social viewpoint. The gifts given by the Spirit in Corinth involve the danger that the unity of the community there will be disrupted. Paul in no way minimizes the gifts of the Spirit; on the contrary, he sees in them an expression of living faith. He emphasizes, however, that these

gifts must be inserted into the whole of the Christian life in such
a way as to build up the whole community and to promote the
growth of faith, hope, and love. Otherwise they would contradict
their own meaning and origin. For it is one and the same Spirit
who has called forth the various gifts in the community. In
bestowing the gifts the Spirit is completely free and sovereign.
Since he is one in himself, the various gifts bestowed by him form
a unity. Paul illuminates this thesis about the unity of gifts
through a comparison. As the human body is one and yet has
many members, all the members, however, forming only one
body, so also Christ. Paul obviously wants to present the union of
believers in Christ in such a way that in place of the expected
word "Spirit," the word "Christ" can be inserted. According to
Paul the baptized form a community in the Spirit. They form one
body, not their own, but the Body of Christ (1 Cor. 12,12). Christ
and the Spirit are the basis of unity for this one body effected by
baptism, for this one society of believers created in baptism.

   One can ask, in regard to the First Epistle to the Corinthians,
whether Paul arrived at his idea of the Church as the Body of
Christ through the idea of the eucharistic body of Christ, or
through the fable which likened the state to an organism, or from
the gnostic concept of primitive man. The comparison made in
the above-cited passage from Corinthians could refer to the fable
of Menenius Agrippa in which he compares the state with a body,
but Paul goes farther when he calls the faithful not only a body
but the body of Christ (1 Cor. 12,27; Eph. 1,23; 4,12; 5,29; Col.
1,24). It is more likely that the origin of the concept lies in the
eucharistic liturgy, because the word "body" is not used by Paul
as a genus, specified by the phrase "of Christ," but rather means
an association with Christ. So it would appear that the concept of
body used in the fable is somewhat changed if that is what is in
the background of Paul's thinking. The Christians form one body,
which is that of Christ, and as parts of this body they are
members of one another.

   The twelfth chapter of 1 Corinthians is closely related to what
Paul says in the letter to the Romans (12,1–8). But in Romans he
goes beyond all that has been said above, insofar as he calls the
believers formally one body "in Christ." That means that the
believers in Rome, as representatives of all the faithful, form an

inner unity, and that this union has its special character from the fact that they are a unity in Christ. The basis of the unity is Christ himself, his saving power and works.

In the letters to the Ephesians and Colossians the Church is referred to as the "body of Christ," while the expression "body in Christ" is missing; Christ is also called the head of the Church (Col. 1,18; Eph. 1,22; 4,15). The letter to the Ephesians calls the Church the mystery of Christ because in it the eternal plan of God, embracing all men, both Jews and Gentiles, is fulfilled. Since God gave Jesus Christ to the Church as head, through whom he created and reconciled all, the Church which is his body, whose fullness fills up all in all (Eph. 1,22f.; Col. 1,18–20), appears as "a heavenly reality filled with divine power. Through it the saving work of Christ occurs, to which it owes its beginning (Eph. 2,13–16; 5,25ff.; Col. 1,20ff.) and in which, in a united humanity, it has its end."[2]

The existence of the Church belongs, therefore, to the eschatological, salvific action of Jesus. A certain nuance of meaning appears in the fact, first, that in the major epistles the faithful are called members of Christ, while in the two letters from prison the Church is called the body of Christ; and, secondly, in the fact that in the former the local church is referred to first of all, and only afterwards the universal Church, while in the latter the universal Church is spoken of immediately. In his explanation of the Church as Body of Christ, the apostle has, in these two letters even more than in the major letters, a paranetic object in view. From the unity of the Christians with Christ and with one another he derives the rules for the perfect Christian life. The word "head" is to be understood, according to the usage of that time, in a twofold sense. The head is the source of life and also the symbol for Christ as the Master, as Lord of the Church.

The Church as the Bride of Christ

From the Old Testament background, Paul develops still another image of the Church, namely that of the Bride of Christ. In the

---

[2]F. Schmid, "Kirche," in H. Fries, *Handbuch Theologischer Grundbegriffe*, I, 793.

Old Testament the relation of God to his People is often presented under the image of the marriage bond. Hosea created this image (chs. 1–3). Ezekiel presents it clearly and in detail (chs. 6 and 23). Isaiah sketches the picture of the beloved who is received again by God with eternal mercy (Is. 54,4–8; 16,5; cf. also the Song of Songs as well as Ps. 64). The union of man and woman as described in Genesis is, according to Paul, a figure of the relation between Christ and the Church (cf. the Council of Vienne, DS 901). He modifies the Old Testament picture in that he refers it not to God but to Jesus Christ. In 2 Corinthians he describes his own activity as that of the spiritual father of the community in Corinth, thinking of his spiritual daughter, the Christian community there, to present her as a chaste virgin to her bridegroom, Christ. The moment of her entrance into the house of the bridegroom is the Parousia. Her virginity consists, according to the description of the apostle, in the purity and integrity of her faith. In Ephesians, Paul elaborates this concept (5,21–33): the Church is the Spouse of Christ. Through his death Christ raised her up to be bride and spouse (Eph. 5,2; Gal. 2,20; 1 Tim. 2,6; Tit. 2,14). The surrender of Jesus Christ to his bride in the crucifixion, in the resurrection and sending of the Spirit, is not an act done once and ended. It never ceases, since his love never tires of giving itself. He lives always for his bride; he cherishes and protects her as his own self; he nourishes her with the strength of his word, above all with his body and blood in the Eucharist. Since he gives her his body and blood, he becomes really one body with her. The union between Christ and the Church surpasses the marriage union in intimacy, strength, and permanence. The union of man and wife is an image of the union between Christ and the Church.

Finally, it is the everlasting divine Love in his own Person—that is, the Holy Spirit—with whom Christ binds the Church to himself. The bride shares in the glory of Christ, but it is a glory not yet apparent. In the Parousia, Christ will come from heaven to meet his bride and unite her with himself. The eschatological meaning of the image of bride is put forward in Ephesians 5,31 and 2 Corinthians 11,2, but it becomes especially clear in the closing chapter of Revelation (19,7–9). Here is described the marriage of the Lamb, for which the bride—that is, the community of the elect—has adorned herself. With great longing her spirit calls "Come." And she hears the answer: "Yes, I am coming soon" (Rev. 22,7.20; 21,2.9). Then the eternal marriage of the Lamb is celebrated (Rev. 19,6–9; 21,2.9).

The Second Vatican Council, in the Constitution on the Church (#7), draws the following inferences from the idea of the Church as community with Christ:

All the members ought to be molded into Christ's image until He is formed in them (cf. Gal. 4,19). For this reason we who have been made like unto Him, who have died with Him and been raised up with Him, are taken up into the mysteries of His life, until we reign together with Him (cf. Phil. 3,21; 2 Tim. 2,11; Eph. 2,6; Col. 2,12, etc.). Still in pilgrimage upon the earth, we travel the paths He trod in trials and under oppression. Made one with His sufferings as the body is one with the head, we endure with Him, that with Him we may be glorified (cf. Rom. 8,17).

◄ 6

The Spirit in the Church

Jesus Christ is present in the Church through his Spirit. Christ and the Spirit are not two realities side by side, or two acting subjects joined in a unity of action. Although they are two "persons," they are a single acting subject, insofar as Christ is active in the Holy Spirit, that is, in the personal Love (in the Love which is a person) in which he forms a single We with the Father.

THE FACT OF HIS PRESENCE

What the Holy Spirit did for the formation of the Church in its beginning he continues to do down through the course of history. He is forever active as the One Sent of the heavenly Father, as the Gift which Jesus Christ has made to his Church, his Body. We know of the abiding efficacy of the Holy Spirit from the promise which is referred to in the gospel of John (cf. Jn. 14,18–24; 14,15–17; 15,26f.; 16,5–15). We can come to know his dynamism in the effective action attested to in the Acts of the Apostles (see, e.g., Acts 4,1–22; 6,3; 6,5f.; 7,51; 7,55; 8,29.39; 10,19; 10,29; 13,9; 13,2; 16,7). According to the Acts, it is the Spirit who gives the final commission to bring God's salvation to the Gentiles (Acts 28,28). The Council of the Apostles is a prime instance of the work of the Holy Spirit (Acts 15,28).

The chief function of the Spirit is the witness to Jesus Christ (Lk. 24,44–49; Acts 1,4–8). It is of the greatest importance,

59

however, to realize that the Holy Spirit bears this witness through men. Hence the testimony of the Holy Spirit assumes the shape of human witness. This appears with special prominence in the inspired Scriptures and in the Church's dogmas. But on this subject what is most important has been said earlier. The operation of the Holy Spirit in the Church is universal. The Holy Spirit is active not only in the officials but in all the members of the Church.

THE MODES OF THE SPIRIT'S OPERATION

A threefold mode of operation can be distinguished. One is seen in the extraordinary, unusual, unexpected working of the Spirit, as described for us in the twelfth chapter of 1 Corinthians. The second type of operation is seen in the daily life of Christians, especially in their mutual unselfish love and in their readiness to take up the cross of the Lord. The third type is found in the official activity of the office-holders appointed by Christ.

Concerning the first type of activity, it would be too narrow an interpretation to reserve this working of the Spirit either to the laity or to the hierarchy. It is confined neither to the one nor to the other, but can extend to all the members of the Christian community, as we see from the description in the letter to the Corinthians. This manifestation of the Spirit, usually designated as "charism," was characteristic of the church in Corinth. It was of special importance for that period in the Church, although it has not been absent in any century. The witness to Christ through such gifts goes beyond the ordinary forms of life in its power. The charismatics are a disturbing element in the Church's life. They could be called the spiritual nonconformists. They are, in a certain sense, identical with those whom we call "saints," insofar as we understand by sanctity not an interior disposition but something breaking forth from the interior, an activity breaking forth out of love. The saints are not comfortable, either for their neighbors or for the entire Church, for they are the enemies of a self-satisfied Christianity. But for this very reason they are indispensable for the true Christian life.

On the one hand, charism is essential for the Christian life in the Spirit of God; on the other hand, it is extremely difficult to recognize. Since false prophets can also appear in the clothing of true, a discernment of spirits is necessary. Christ said that the mark of the true prophet is the fruit which he brings forth. Vatican Council II speaks of the danger of subjectivity and assigns to the hierarchy the duty of "proving" the spirit (Constitution on the Church, #12; cf. 1 Thess. 5,12.19–21).

Despite these critical observations, it still remains of the greatest importance for the life of faith in the Church that there shall always be charismatic figures in it, so that its life does not grow sterile. Scripture also declares that the Church was built upon the foundation of the apostles and prophets (Eph. 2,19ff.); and by prophets is understood those who are driven in a special way by the Holy Spirit, who consume themselves in the service of their brothers. Charismatic persons have the responsibility, of course, to set themselves within the order of the whole in such a way that the unity of the community is not lessened. But as, on the one hand, charisms create a danger that right order will be disturbed, so, on the other hand, through the stifling of charisms, right order can be so exaggerated that the result is the peace of a cemetery. Paul sees this last danger when in the First Epistle to the Thessalonians he says: "Do not stifle inspiration" (1 Thess. 5,19).

As far as the everyday working of the Holy Spirit is concerned, it brings about both the readiness to witness to Christ and the understanding of the witness. The operation of the Spirit is described for us as a strengthening, a consoling, an enlightening, an opening of the heart; as an encounter by which man sees into his sinful condition and turns away from it toward Christ (Acts 2,40; 9,31; 11,22f.; 13,15; 14,14; Rom. 8,28–30; 12,8; 1 Cor. 14,3; 2 Cor. 8,4.17; Heb. 3,7; 12,5; 1 Tim. 4,13). The Holy Spirit enables man to say a yes in faith to Christ as to his master. It is only in the Spirit that this yes can be spoken (1 Cor. 12,13; 1 Jn. 4,2–3; 1 Cor. 2,12–15; Eph. 1,17–18). The Spirit gives to the human spirit, in its innermost self, the witness to the fact that he is the Son of God (Rom. 8,16; 1 Jn. 3,19–24). He prays, in man's own person, with inexpressible sighs, when man himself is dumb before God (Rom. 8,26f.; 1 Jn. 2,20–27; Jn. 16,13).

The apostle Peter sees in the outpouring of the Spirit its fulfillment of the Old Testament prophecies, to which he calls attention in his speech on Pentecost. The Spirit works in the office-holders. If Christ also prepared the ministries in the Church, yet it is in the sending of the Spirit that they become effective. Thus the official, juridical element in the Church is an effect of the Spirit and for that reason cannot be in opposition to the charismatic element. The operation of the Spirit is expressed not only in the charismatic event but also in the institutional element.[1] The Spirit is the principle not only of freedom but also of authority (or office). As life principle of the Church he unifies the official and unofficial. This abiding efficacy of the Holy Spirit is explained as follows in the Constitution on the Church (#4):

When the work which the Father had given the Son to do on earth (cf. Jn. 17,4) was accomplished, the Holy Spirit was sent on the day of Pentecost in order that He might forever sanctify the Church, and thus all believers would have access to the Father through Christ in the one Spirit (cf. Eph. 2,18). He is the Spirit of life, a fountain of water springing up to life eternal (cf. Jn. 4,14; 7,38–39). Through Him the Father gives life to men who are dead from sin, till at last He revives in Christ even their mortal bodies (cf. Rom. 8,10–11).

The Spirit dwells in the Church and in the hearts of the faithful as in a temple (cf. 1 Cor. 3,16; 6,19). In them he prays and bears witness to the fact that they are adopted sons (cf. Gal. 4,6; Rom. 8,15–16 and 26). The Spirit guides the Church into the fullness of truth (cf. Jn. 16,13) and gives her a unity of fellowship and service. He furnishes and directs her with various gifts, both hierarchical and charismatic, and adorns her with the fruits of His grace (cf. Eph. 4,11–12; 1 Cor. 12,4; Gal. 5,22). By the power of the gospel He makes the Church grow, perpetually renews her, and leads her to perfect union with her Spouse. The Spirit and the Bride both say to the Lord Jesus, "Come" (cf. Apoc. 22,17).

It is under these aspects that all believers in Christ can and must be called "spiritual" men.

[1]L.-L. Leube, *L'institution et l'evenement* (Neuchatel, 1950).

ANALOGY WITH THE INCARNATION

With regard to the mode of presence of the Spirit in the Church, Cardinal Manning made the suggestion at the First Vatican Council that the relationship of the Holy Spirit can be clarified by analogy with the incarnation, although one cannot in any sense speak of a hypostatic union. Actually the Fathers of the Church often try to illustrate the relation in which the Spirit stands to the Church by means of a comparison with the incarnation of the Logos. This comparison is capable of casting light on the relation of the Holy Spirit to the Church, but only up to a point. As has already been stressed, there is no hypostatic union between the Holy Spirit and the Church. The Church does not belong to the Holy Spirit as to the divine *suppositum* which bears it, as the human nature of Jesus Christ belongs to the divine Logos as the person bearing it. Between the Spirit and the Church there is no unity of existence, only a unity of action. It should also be noted that whereas the human nature which Jesus assumed in his divine existence is individual, the Holy Spirit is bound to the whole of mankind. He is primarily a societal spirit. The individual believers who are united in the community of the Church in the Holy Spirit preserve their selfhood, even while they are changed into a new and divine creation. They are not united in a mystical universal nature, whose ground of subsistence is the Holy Spirit. Spirit and Church are not absorbed together in a pantheistic unity. The Spirit of Jesus dwells in the Church and in its members. Also, when the human nature of Jesus acts, it is an action of God. This cannot be said in the same sense of the Church, where the independence of man has a much greater scope. Although the human nature of Jesus Christ also has responsibility and spontaneity, in the relation of the Church to the Holy Spirit these characteristics have not a greater but a different quality.

For this reason one can say that the Church is determined in its outward manifestations essentially by the behavior of men, both through the human characteristics of individuals, especially of its leaders such as the pope and bishops, and through the human groups, the nations and races which compose it. This impress does not have a purely external meaning, but pertains to the actual realization in time of the Church, penetrated by the Holy Spirit.

For a more precise understanding we can make the following distinction. The Church can be considered either as the community of those believing in Christ (*Heilsgemeinschaft*) or as the societal institution through which salvation is bestowed (*Heilsanstalt*). It is both in one, but either aspect can be separately emphasized. When the Church is considered as the community of believers, the freedom of the individual is more prominent. Insofar as it is an institution for offering salvation, the Holy Spirit uses the empowered members of the Church as instruments of his sanctifying operation. What those who are employed by him as instruments do is not done primarily for themselves but for others. They can freely make themselves available for the operation of the Spirit, but they cannot determine the content of that operation, although they are free as to the manner of presentation of that content, and to that extent can exercise their own human individuality. The situation is different when the Church is considered as the community of those believing in Christ, of those saved by faith. In this case also the Holy Spirit is the one who works, and he does it through grace indwelling in the faithful. But what he does in this case serves the salvation of those possessed by the Holy Spirit himself. They can open themselves to him to a greater or lesser degree. They can flee from his initiative and go back to their own human weakness, or they can open to him unreservedly.

THE HOLY SPIRIT AS THE SOUL
OF THE CHURCH

Since the time of Augustine the relation of the Church to the Holy Spirit has been expressed by the statement that the Spirit is the soul of the Church, that is, its life principle. This formulation, developed in theology, has been taken up in the texts of the Second Vatican Council. The Holy Spirit is united to the Church as the soul is to the body. But the analogous character of this expression must be emphasized. The image is meant to signify that the Church is what it is through the Holy Spirit. Through the Spirit it becomes its "I"; in him it attains its selfhood. In this sense the Church is understood as a quasi-personal being, as a community which is a quasi-person and which becomes this particularly through the fact that Christ is its head. The Holy Spirit, of whom it is said that he is given to the Church, that he abides in the Church, that he is present in it—dwells in it, fulfills it, prays and teaches in it, leads it—endows the Church with life, movement, and efficacy. On the other hand, Spirit and Church are not united, as are the body and soul, into a unified, substantial whole. If it is true that whatever happens in the Church—so far as it is really an event of the Church—is the work of the Spirit, it is also the doing of men. Here we must move from logical to dialectical expressions. The Spirit is not reduced to a oneness with the community. He does not become one element in the unified diversity of the faithful. Just as there is no christological pantheism, so there is no pantheism of the Spirit. Perhaps we could express the relation of the Holy Spirit to the Church analogously with the mystery of the Trinity and the incarnation in the formulation of H. Muhlen: "One person in many persons."

THE CHURCH AS COVENANT OF LOVE

It should be emphasized that the relation of the Holy Spirit to the Church is especially determined by the fact that the Spirit is the Love within the Godhead. The Church must be a community of love. Love is the deepest mystery of the Church. The Church is a covenant of love, not through the alliance of its members, but as a dispensation arranged by the love of God. The Church is given for the individual, but it is also the brotherhood in which individuals are united. So it is the gift of love from above and the answer of love from below; or from a historical viewpoint, handed down and always newly creating the community of love. This is the quality of the Church which is referred to when it is spoken of in Scripture as the brotherhood.

The characteristic of the Church as a covenant of love is not contradicted by the fact that it is hierarchically constituted, that there are command and obedience in it. For the love of God conferred on men makes this obligatory. Every divine self-communication imposes a duty and a responsibility on man. This love can be a burden for him, just as an earthly love can. It represents a requirement that man rise out of his sins and shortcomings to surrender himself to God. Thus love assumes the form of a commandment, an obligation.

◄ III

The Development
of Ecclesiology

◄7

Overview of the History of Ecclesiology

It has often been pointed out, and rightly, that theological reflection about the Church, as well as dogmatic statements of the Church about itself, have been crystallized only in our own day. The fact is, however, that practically all the elements of ecclesiology have been the object of theological development as well as of Church definition and proclamation through the centuries. It is only today that these individual elements have been brought together into a whole. Following Yves Congar's treatment of this subject, we will trace the development through the three periods: the age of the Fathers to the seventh century (Isidore), the Middle Ages, and the modern era.

THE AGE OF THE FATHERS

For the conception of the Church in the second century it is of fundamental importance that the writings left behind by the apostles were appended to the sacred writings of the Old Testament, so that together they formed "the Holy Scripture" (the Canon). The biblical writings arising under divine inspiration became for the Church, from the second century on, its basic law, a conscious reflection of itself, to which it was bound for the entire future. In these writings the reality of the Church was

69

delineated, as it was constituted in baptism, in faith, in the Eucharist, in the society of believers, and in the office-holders, who direct the life of the Church. This life is holy in its totality. Although occasionally incipient heresies were attacked by Irenaeus, Cyprian, and Augustine, the Fathers were for the most part interpreters of the Scriptures—which, however, were still far removed from providing a systematic ecclesiology. Their interpretations refer to the images used for the Church in Scripture—a people, a body, the temple, a house, a bride, a flock, a vineyard, a Jerusalem above, the holy city, a field, a net. They arrange these pictures into a great typological kingdom, in which they compare the Church with paradise, with heaven, with the dove, the moon, a ship, the Ark, the rock without fissure, and with many biblical persons such as Eve, Adam, Mary Magdalen, or Mary the Mother of Jesus. From this stems a rich ecclesiological symbolism which is more useful for religious edification than for theological inquiry. So there arose "the picture of a Church which fasts and prays, is attacked, does penance, is converted, strives against the demons, and reaches the high-point of its self-realization in the saints, in the martyrs, in the virgins, in the ascetics, and in the monks" (Congar).[1]

Not without some influence from a basic neo-Platonic frame of mind (although this is *not* a new-platonic train of thought), the Church was interpreted as a sacramental sign in which the heavenly reality is so bound up with the earthly symbolism that God communicates his salvation to mankind through the sign as through an earthly organ. The danger here, of course, is that the concept of the Church may be affected by a Platonic ontology according to which true being is the invisible, while the visible is only a shadow, an improper kind of being. Augustine particularly had to fight against this danger. If he did not overcome it, he always submerged it in the eschatological vision presented in the New Testament, according to which the present world is subject to the past, but always reaches forward and out toward an

---

[1] *The Meaning of Tradition*, trans. A. N. Woodrow (New York, Hawthorn Books, 1964).

everlasting existence. Here the neo-Platonic vertical is transformed into the Christian horizontal.

The most significant contribution of the patristic era is that generally, although not without exception, the Church is seen as the society of Christians, as that totality in which unity and charity endure (the communion of saints). The Church exercises a spiritual motherhood. It is important to keep in mind that those centuries saw the development of the idea of apostolicity and apostolic succession in the Church (Irenaeus), of the importance of the bishop and of the bishops' councils (Cyprian), of the idea of the living relation of the Church to the whole world (theology of the Greek Fathers) and the independence of the Church from the power of the state (Augustine), while at the same time the concept of salvation by force, of the use of the worldly sword (Augustine, Isidore) also emerged. Augustine evolved a theology in which apostolicity was intrinsically bound up with catholicity and in which the validity of sacramental efficacy was established as independent from the person of the individual minister, so preparing the doctrine of the sacramental character. After a short prologue in the second century, the bishops of Rome from the third century to the fifth century developed the theory of the primacy of the bishop of Rome. This theology was brought to a conclusion by Leo the Great (d. 461).

THE MIDDLE AGES

In considering the further development of these theological ideas, it is extremely important to keep in mind that from the time of Constantine the Church occupied an influential position within the empire. From the time of Charlemagne the Church was understood as the whole body of Christians; as a consequence Charlemagne called himself the head of the Church and issued laws for the regulation of Church matters. But under his weaker successors the bishops regained their influence and again took over the actual direction of the Church. Parallel with this came the building up of an ever stronger concentration of ecclesiastical power in the hands of the pope. In the middle of the ninth century began the break between the Western and Eastern Churches under the patriarch Photius. As a result the Catholic Church had thereafter only a Western destiny and a Western countenance.

Under Gregory VII the battle over the freedom of the Church was fought, and appeal to the direct establishment of the papal power through God was settled. The papal power was understood to this effect, that the pope had the full power to depose kings if these infringed the rights of God and the Church. In this encounter the papacy achieved one of its most momentous victories. On the one hand, this meant for the earthly society the beginning of secularization; on the other hand, the Church regained its original and proper character as an independent spiritual society. At the same time this development led to the idea that the papacy is the "head, base, root, fount, and source" of all power and authority in the Church. The Church is considered to be founded in the papal power and derived from it (*Dictatus Papae* and various decrees). It was just this concept of the papacy which had the effect of making final the division of East from West.

The inner life of the Church showed a great strength at this time. Scholasticism began to develop at the beginning of the eleventh century. The sign of the cross covered the spiritual horizon. Strong lay movements arose, many of them, however, with an anti-Church bias (neo-Manichaeism, the Waldensians, the "Catholic Poor," the eremitic life, as well as monasticism itself). A meaningful appreciation for the worth of the individual developed together with a new sense of social solidarity (the communal movement in the twelfth century). There also arose an explicit and strong sense of order which found expression in the different states of life, especially in the monastic state and in the married state.

From the middle of the twelfth century onwards the Church was interpreted from the christological aspect of the mystical body of Christ. It is especially Thomas Aquinas who sees the Church in its relationship to Christ in such a manner that he describes Christ as the Head of the Church and speaks of the grace of Christ as the "grace of the Head." This view signifies a change insofar as the Church until then had been interpreted as the true body of Christ in a eucharistic sense, as the expression "mystical body" signifies. However, in the time of Thomas the Church was far from being seen only in a christological or incarnational sense. The spirit-element, so strongly emphasized by Augustine, was not lacking. Augustine, we know, taught that if one has part in the body of Christ, one lives also from the spirit of Christ. Thus Scholasticism consisted of a number of different elements. The Church was understood as the congregation of the believers who are united through Christ in faith, or as the body of Christ insofar as it is animated and instructed by this spirit.

However, a real treatise on the Church was not produced in this period. Such a treatise did begin to take shape, especially through the encounter with the sects of the Waldensians and the Cathari and in the controversies between the kings and the pope—that between Philip the Fair and Boniface VIII in particular. But these treatises are confined to particular problems, following the trends of the times. In these controversies the phrase, the "indirect power" of the Church was introduced. At the time of the Great Western Schism there developed another movement directly opposed to that of the papal primacy, namely the Conciliar Movement. The general trend of ideas in the reform of Gregory the Great, which made the Church completely dependent on the papacy, was completely reversed by one which went to the opposite extreme. According to the Conciliar Theory, only a council can judge the legitimacy of the claims of two contenders for the papacy, and such a council must, if necessary, be convoked independently of the pope. The conciliar decrees of Basel and Constance, and of course also the theses of John Hus, were the occasion for the first real theological treatises on the Church (John of Ragusa and above all John of Turr).

MODERN TIMES

A new development set in with the Reformation, which called into question the institutional and authoritarian element in the Church. According to the Reformers, the Church is the society of the true believers, but invisible and known only to God. In the relationship of mankind to God only the authority of God and his word is binding. Church authority rests on a purely human, social and practical expediency. All the baptized are equally priests. The Council of Trent rejected many of the theses of the Reformers; but with regard to ecclesiology it emphasized only the idea of a special priesthood. It was Robert Bellarmine who gave the response to the Reformers' ecclesiology. His work on the Church was accepted as to some extent official, and later it became the source for numerous treatises on ecclesiology, even down to our own day. Bellarmine offers an apologetic of the Church based on its signs, or "marks." In the seventeenth and eighteenth centuries, the authority of the teaching Church and the problem of the papacy were the foremost objects of discussion in controversies over Protestant theology, Gallicanism, Febronianism, and Episcopalism. Ecclesiology more and more restricted the idea of the Church to that of a visible, hierarchically ordered, supernatural, complete or "perfect" society.

In the nineteenth century there were two streams of thought which came after the breakthroughs of the Enlightenment and the French Revolution (and of Josephinism, of Febronianism) and helped to shape the further development of ecclesiology. One attempted to support the papal authority (in France and Italy); the other attempted to renew the Catholic spirit, and through a fresh exposition of Scripture and the Fathers to attain to a new outlook on the Church. This last was the work of Johann Adam Möhler more than any other. While Möhler concerned himself first of all with a spirit-centered ecclesiology, he achieved in his *Symbolik* a synthesis of the christocentric and pneumocentric. Möhler's ecclesiology influenced the thinking of Franzelin and Schrader, the Jesuit theologians who, with Perrone, revised the constitutions of the First Vatican Council. A constitution on the Church based on the idea of the mystical body had been prepared for the First Vatican Council. It did not, however, find approval in the Council, which limited itself to defining the primacy of the pope and defending it against conciliar views.

In the first half of our century ecclesiology received a great impetus, in Protestant as well as Catholic theology. It was O. Dibelius who said that the twentieth century is the century of the Church; and Romano Guardini, writing in 1922, expressed it thus:

"A religious process of incalculable significance has set in, the Church is awakening in souls." A whole series of movements led to the new interest in ecclesiology: the biblical movement, the liturgical movement, research in patristics, the ecumenical movement, and also the questions of the Church's relationship to the non-Catholic Christian Churches and of the salvation of men living outside the Catholic or Christian faith. Today's ecclesiology is characterized by its biblical and ecumenical orientation, and in this connection there arises the question of the relation of the Church to the world in the widest sense—to its culture and economy, to society, to politics, to art, to science.

‹ 8

The Church's Official Doctrine about Itself

Parallel to this development in theological thinking stands the Church's official teaching about itself. First of all, the early creeds express in a simple, straightforward way the faith of the Church in itself and in its fundamental attributes (catholicity, apostolicity, unity). Then reflection begins upon individual elements of the Church's self-understanding, for example, on the primacy of the pope (Second Council of Lyons, DS 861; Council of Florence, DS 1307; cf. DS 1454). In the process of this self-reflection the ecclesiological spiritualism of Wyclif and Hus was rejected (Council of Constance, DS 1109, 1164, 1180, 1187, 1191, 1194, 1201f.).

The Reformation gave a powerful impetus to the understanding of the Church. It caused the institutional and hierarchical elements especially, as well as the special priesthood and the office of bishop—although not the primacy of the pope—to be emphasized. The chief ecclesiological achievement of the Council of Trent was to open the way, through its definitions of justification, of the meaning of faith, and of the sacraments, for a predominantly structural conception of the Church. When, in the nineteenth century, the Church set about forming a general doctrine of ecclesiology over against the dangers threatening her from movements of the most varied kinds, only a partial success was

76

achieved, for different reasons both internal and external. The principal development was the definition of papal primacy. The ecclesiological interpretations undertaken since the First Vatican Council reached their climax in Pius XII's encyclical *Mystici Corporis* of June 29, 1943.

For the Second Vatican Council the central problem was the understanding of the Church, not only for the members of the Church itself but also in relation to non-Catholic Christians and to non-Christians—in fact, to the whole world of today. The outcome of the conciliar endeavors is found in the Dogmatic Constitution on the Church (*Lumen Gentium*) of November 21, 1964. For a comprehensive interpretation of the Church's teaching here, we must take in combination with this Constitution the Council's decree on the Bishops' Pastoral Office in the Church, together with the decrees on the Missions, on the Eastern Churches, on Ecumenism, and on the Laity. The Constitution on the Church is of the greatest significance because it is the first official document in which an overall view of the Church is presented—in this case, under the key concept of the Church as the People of God. Pius XII's encyclical and the Constitution of the Second Vatican Council, taken together, run counter to the divided thinking which had developed in ecclesiology in post-Tridentine theology (distinguishing between the body and the soul of the Church, between institution and society, between the institutional "it" and the societal "we"). In post-Tridentine thinking the legal element was understood as the proper ecclesial domain, an element which had only a loose relationship with the salvation-mediating function of the Church. In this view the concept of the Church was of a complete or "perfect" society with its own authority, derived from natural law. This view overlooked the fact that the Church is an instrument of Christ and the Spirit, and has only a delegated authority (K. Mörsdorf).

THE CATHOLIC CHURCH'S UNDERSTANDING OF ITSELF

Underlying all the differences between the Catholic and the Protestant understanding of the Church today there is the question of unity. Unity, for example, is central to this statement, that "the Church essentially appertains to the will of Christ and the gospel; that the Church is the People of God and the body of Christ, visible in its signs; that it is one, holy, catholic, and apostolic; that as an eschatological reality it is the beginning of a new world to come; and that it has a mission embracing the entire world."[1]

The differences concern elements of no little consequence, although they are insignificant when put alongside those between Christian and non-Christian religions. The differences can be briefly enumerated. The Orthodox understanding is "the image of an absolute Church of the three divine Persons." It has its source, according to Bulgakov, beyond space and time, in the divine wisdom. Since Pentecost, Christ continues through the Church the salvation of the world. He is the head of the whole Church. In this no bishop can represent him although in the liturgy the local bishop can take the place of Christ at the table, in order to entreat the Spirit's descent upon the offerings and the people. Only the first seven general councils are recognized by the Orthodox Church, and only one dogma—the trinitarian. The Church is one in the apostolic tradition as *Koinonia*. The Papal primacy in particular is rejected.

According to the Lutheran concept, the Church is the new People of God, created through the Word of God and perpetually grounded in it, the congregation or communion of the saints, that is, of the faithful. The trinitarian God is present in his Word, and there he accomplishes our salvation as Creator, as Savior, and as the one who gives life. Where God's Word is, there the kingdom of God prevails. This kingdom is always at war with the kingdom of the devil. True apostolic authority is given by fidelity to the witness of the Scriptures. This authority is exercised where Scripture is taught and proclaimed in its pure form. For this purpose the offices of bishop, of pastor, and of teacher are indispensable. Union with the Word is not, however, dependent on official apostolic succession, and in particular not on the

---

[1]K. E. Skydsgaard's article on the Church in *LTK*, Vol. 6, 183.

papacy. The Word is its own divine guarantee. The living Word of God, received in faith, is the essential basis of union.

The Calvinist concept of the Church is characterized by an emphasis on predestination, on ecclesiastical discipline, and a manifold ministry. Holy Scripture is the only authority, for the individual as well as for the community.

In the eighteenth and nineteenth centuries various movements arose within Protestantism. There was an effort to revivify the Lutheran teaching; in some areas Protestantism grew into a religious individualism or pietism; elsewhere it grew into an attempt to identify the Church and the kingdom of God with secular culture. After the first World War, European Protestantism developed a new conception of itself under the influence of Karl Barth, especially, and the struggle against Hitler. New insights from biblical scholarship and the encounter with the Catholic Church created a new situation. The dialogue in which the Catholic Church is trying to find elements of the true Church in the Protestant groups and the Protestant Church is seeking to find such elements in the Catholic Church has proved fruitful. Yet the ecumenical movement still has far to go, and there is a temptation for Church officials to indulge in a form of public ecumenism which leaves their own house untouched.

◄ IV

The Structure
of the Church

The Church is one—there are not many Churches—and the one Church of Christ is organically structured. In this section we shall discuss the two problems of the uniqueness of the Church and its unity. A closely related problem is the question of the necessity of the Church for salvation. Insofar as this latter question concerns the salvation of the individual we shall touch upon it here; as it concerns the ecclesiastical status of the Church community it will be discussed separately in Volume V, on the Church's sacramentality.

‹9

The Uniqueness of the Church: Catholicity and Visibility

The Church is the efficacious sign of the saving will of God, which is directed toward all men. As there was only one People of God in the Old Testament, so also in the New Testament there is only one, the Church. Christ has only one Mystical Body, only one Bride. The words of the letter to the Ephesians hold good: "One body and one spirit, as you are called in one hope of your calling. One Lord, one faith, one baptism, one God and Father of all, who is over all and through all and in all" (4,5). The uniqueness of the Church corresponds to the uniqueness of God; to the uniqueness of the Mediator sent by him, his representative among men and of men before God; to the uniqueness of the Holy Spirit. Jesus Christ has entrusted all salvation to the one Church which he has prepared.

Two or more Churches in this sense would be pointless. The one head, Christ, has only one body; the one bridegroom has only one bride. There is only one Lord and one faith and one baptism (DS 870ff.). Leo XIII taught the same doctrine, and the Second Vatican Council expressed the same idea many times. The Constitution on the Church (#8) states:

Christ, the one Mediator, established and ceaselessly sustains here of earth His holy Church, the community of faith, hope, and charity, as

83

a visible structure. Through her He communicates truth and grace to all. But the society furnished with hierarchical agencies and the Mystical Body of Christ are not to be considered as two realities, nor are the visible assembly and the spiritual community, nor the earthly Church and the Church enriched with heavenly things. Rather they form one interlocked reality which is comprised of a divine and human element. . . .

This is the unique Church of Christ which in the Creed we avow as one, holy, catholic, and apostolic. After his Resurrection our Savior handed her over to Peter to be shepherded (Jn. 21,17), commissioning him and the other apostles to propagate and govern her (cf. Mt. 28,18ff.). Her he erected for all ages as "the pillar and mainstay of the truth" (1 Tim. 3,15). This Church, constituted and organized in the world as a society, subsists in the Catholic Church, which is governed by the successor Peter and by the bishops in union with that successor, . . . "

(See also the Decree on Ecumenism, Ch. I, #2.)

This text teaches that the one Church willed by Christ and forever animated by the presence of his Spirit is to be found as a concrete reality. It takes visible form in the Catholic Church, but not with a visibility like that possessed by material things. Its visibleness still contains a hiddenness, a mystery. The Church of Christ is visible in its instruments, in the bishops, in the pope, in its proclamation of the Word, in its dispensing of the sacraments. That it is really the Church of Jesus Christ, and not just any kind of religious society, can only be affirmed in faith. The condition of the Church members with regard to salvation is invisible. So, despite all its visible signs, the Church remains finally—that is, in its Christ-mystery—invisible and accessible only to faith. In this she is like her head, Jesus. In him also the divine was visible in the man Jesus, but for anyone who did not look to him with the eyes of faith, the divinity remained invisible and inscrutable.

The one Church must be the efficacious sign of God's saving mercy for all men; in other words, it must be catholic, or universal.

Catholicity is necessarily bound up with oneness. The catholicity of the Church, which is confessed in all the creeds, can be seen both as an exterior and as an interior quality. Exteriorly, this is to be understood in the sense that it is ordered toward all mankind, to all peoples of all time (catholicity of persons). Interiorly, catholicity consists in the fullness of truth and the grace of salvation (*heilontologische*, "catholicity"). Exterior catholicity means that the Church is not bound to a certain race or culture, or to a particular political or economic form. It is not limited in any such way, but transcends all geographic, national, historic, cultural, and political boundaries. But above all this, catholicity means that the Church has the ability to reach all men and all nations with their individual and collective peculiarities, and is capable of mediating to them what they need for the final fulfillment of their humanity—that is, salvation, peace with God and with one another. Whoever enters the Church of Christ does not need to give up his own natural characteristics. An Indian need not become a European in order to be a Christian. Whoever begins to believe in Christ needs neither to stop being the concrete individual man that he is nor to give up his nationality. In fact, just the reverse should happen: through faith in Christ a man is enabled to become exactly what he is destined to be, to grow beyond his limitations into his true and proper reality. The Church provides him with a power of self-realization which does not come with his purely natural state. She frees him from those forces which stand in the way of his true self-realization. The Church offers to all men—of whatever race, whatever political system, to whatever level of culture they belong—the means to self-development. Through its incorporation into the Church, human nature is freed from the fundamental impediments to its growth.

Exterior catholicity also means that the Church is of such a nature as to extend through all time and space. It has the power to overcome transitoriness. While it must be said of every other phenomenon within history that it has its time—meaning that it comes and goes, that it cannot exist beyond its appointed age—one must say of the Church that its time is always and its place is everywhere. It never becomes antiquated or obsolete. It will never be replaced by a new and better plan of salvation.

The extension through time is not simply a passive continuance; rather it is a dynamic, salvific acting. For the Church has the one salvation, the salvation of Christ, to proclaim in every time and in every place with its different levels of development. It must continually translate its message into a language understandable in the present time. So it is not once and for all finished; it is always an open society. Consequently, despite the essential commonality in the traditional faith, in the liturgy, and in communion with the apostolic see and with the bishops, it appears—or should appear—differently in every age, conditioned by the differences in manner of life, ways of thinking, cultural development; differently in the Far East, in Europe, in America, and in Africa. The liturgical life especially develops differently in different times and places, despite the common center, Jesus Christ. Certain truths of faith acquire a different emphasis, so that one retreats while another comes into the foreground, and all the while the Christ-event remains the central reality. Through the diversity in the living out of the one essentially same faith, through the varied expressions of Christian hope and love, the Church attains its complete fulfillment. The individual communities, small or large, and the local churches combine into the totality of the universal Church; or rather, the universal Church becomes visible in the local churches. The communion of saints as the society of the "holy," and as a society in holiness, particularly through the communal commemoration of the death of its Lord, establishes unity amidst all change through the centuries until the last hour, and over the whole world to the very ends of the earth. But the diversity can, of course, become so great that the danger of division and schism threatens.

The Second Vatican Council worked out very clearly the law and limit of this process. In relation to the catholicity of the one Church of Jesus Christ it declared (Constitution on the Church, #13):

It follows that among all the nations of earth there is but one People of God, which takes its citizens from every race, making them citizens of a kingdom which is of a heavenly and not an earthly nature. For all the faithful scattered throughout the world are in communion with each other in the Holy Spirit, so that "he who occupies the See of Rome knows the people of India are his members." (Cf. St. John Chrysostom, *In Jo.*, Hom. 65, 1.) Since the kingdom of God is not of this world (cf. Jn. 18,36), the Church or People of God takes nothing away from the temporal welfare of any people by establishing that kingdom. Rather does she foster and take to herself, insofar as they are good, the ability, resources, and customs of each people. Taking them to herself she purifies, strengthens, and ennobles them. The Church in this is mindful that she must harvest with that King to whom the nations were given for an inheritance (cf. Ps. 2,8) and into whose city they bring gifts and presents (cf. Ps. 71 [72], 10; Is. 60,4–7; Apoc. 21,24). This characteristic of universality which adorns the People of God is a gift from the Lord Himself. By reason of it, the Catholic Church strives energetically and constantly to bring all humanity with all its riches back to Christ its Head in the unity of His Spirit.

In virtue of this catholicity each individual part of the Church contributes through its special gifts to the good of the other parts and of the whole Church. Thus through the common sharing of gifts and through the common effort to attain fullness in unity, the whole and each of the parts receive increase. Not only, then, is the People of God made up of different peoples but even in its inner structure it is composed of various ranks. This diversity among its members arises either by reason of their duties, as is the case with those who exercise the sacred ministry for the good of their brethren, or by reason of their situation and way of life, as is the case with those many who enter the religious state and, tending toward holiness by a narrower path, stimulate their brethren by their example.

Moreover, within the Church particular Churches hold a rightful place. These Churches retain their own traditions without in any way lessening the primacy of the Chair of Peter. This Chair presides over the whole assembly of charity (cf. St. Ignatius of Antioch, *Ad. Rom.*, Praef.) and protects legitimate differences, while at the same time it sees that such differences do not hinder unity but rather contribute toward it. Finally, between all the parts of the Church there remains a bond of close communion with respect to spiritual riches, apostolic workers, and temporal resources. For the members of the People of God are called to share these goods, and to each of the Churches the words of the Apostle apply: "According to the gift that each has received administer it to one another as good stewards of the manifold grace of God" (1 Pet. 4,10).

All men are called to be part of this catholic unity of the People of God, a unity which is a harbinger of the universal peace it promotes. And there belong to it or are related to it in various ways, the Catholic faithful as well as all who believe in Christ, and indeed the whole of mankind. For all men are called to salvation by the grace of God.

‹ 10

The One Church and the Many Churches

The faith-statement about the unity of the Church quoted in the foregoing chapter evokes a most difficult question. For we know that other Christian communities claim to be the true Church of Christ and to possess the Christian heritage. So there arises the difficult problem as to how the teaching of the Catholic Church on the unity of the Church can be reconciled with the practical situation. The question is important, not only in order to understand the Church rightly but also to clarify the position of the non-Catholic Christian communities and to answer the question of the necessity for salvation of the one Church of Christ. In the time before the Second Vatican Council many attempts were made at a solution. To approach the problem we must distinguish between the membership of an individual and the ecclesiastical status of a church group.

THE TEACHING BEFORE
THE SECOND VATICAN COUNCIL

The "Votum" *of the Church*

The theology of the Middle Ages, on the basis of several very meager statements of the Fathers, formulated a theory of the *votum* of the Church, or *votum* of the sacraments. A *"votum"* in

this sense refers to something that a person would do if he knew
he should, e.g. join the Catholic Church, although in actual fact he
does not do so, because he does not realize that he ought to. This
concept seemed to allow the possibility of salvation for those not
formally belonging to the Church. In that time, of course, the
problem did not have the urgency it has today, for it was believed
that the lands lying around the Mediterranean constituted the
entire world and therefore that the Christian message had already
reached practically all men. But with the discovery of the Far
East and of the New World the theological situation changed
completely, as it became evident that there were large nations to
whose frontiers the Christian message had not yet advanced.
Hence the question of the necessity of the Church for salvation
emerged under a new aspect. As a result, the idea of *votum* was
more strongly delineated. The question was: What is the minimum possible content of the intention or desire, or in what way
must it be developed in order to bring salvation? The most
extreme answer was that the desire had to include at least a
general yearning toward the divine—that is, toward the True and
the Good—and embrace in general the obligations implicit in that.
We find this formulated, after some preliminary theological
theorizing, in the encyclicals *Mediator Dei* and *Mystici Corporis*,
the latter of which immediately precipitated a lively discussion of
the question.

Membership in the "Soul" and in the "Body" of the Church

Many times before, the thesis had been put forward that a
distinction must be made between membership in the soul and in
the body of the Church. The body of the Church is understood
not in the Pauline sense of the community of the Church with
Christ as its head, but as the external organization. The soul is
understood as the interior community of grace. It is membership
in the soul of the Church which suffices for salvation. Such a
distinction is influenced—one can hardly argue the point—by the
Protestant idea of the Church. So it can be said that the Catholic
theologians in the post-Tridentine period made use of the Protestant concept of the Church, although perhaps not consciously, in

order to solve that extraordinarily difficult problem of the necessity of the Church for salvation. From this arose the danger that the external, legal form of the Church would be considered as something purely extrinsic and thus of secondary importance. This was completely rejected by Pius XII, but then from his statement new difficulties arose. It should be pointed out, however, before we go into the interpretation of this text, that in general in this discussion, the question under consideration is of the salvation of the individual, not the ecclesiastical status of the Church community.

The Teaching of Pius XII

Pius XII taught that only those who have been baptized, profess the true faith, and have neither cut themselves off from the body of the Church nor been cut off by legitimate authority because of grave fault are to be counted as full members of the Church. He cites 1 Corinthians 12,13, and then extends the text thus: "It follows that those who are divided in faith or leadership cannot be living in this one body or out of one divine Spirit" (DS 3802).

This text was given two or three different interpretations because of the problem of baptism. According to the statements of the Fathers and the formal teaching of the Council of Florence (Decree *Exsultate Leo* of November 22, 1439), baptism makes us members of Christ and incorporates us into the body of the Church (*de corpore efficimur Ecclesiae*), as already stated by the Third Council of Valencia 855 c.5 (DS 633). According to Pope Benedict XIV, baptism administered outside the Catholic Church also has this effect (DS 2567). This teaching seems to be in irreconcilable conflict with the thesis of Pius XII. It could be said that the traditional teaching about the efficacy of baptism implies the idea of one legitimate Church of Christ. It seems that we must distinguish between an ontological and a dynamic notion of Church membership. The first means, in the phrase of canon law, "to be a person in the Church," and it is effected by baptism. Both the sacramental character and its effect are then ineradicable. Through a prohibition or penalty imposed by a Church official the rights of membership can be curtailed, but the actual membership cannot be taken away. Full membership for the adult Christian exists only when he is not excluded from the life of the community through any prohibition or penalty, when to the actual membership he joins the living of a Christian life.

On the other hand, the dynamic notion allows for degrees of Church membership. While this idea is related to the question of function within the Church, it is also a matter of intensity of life. The theory of degrees of membership is only understandable on the presupposition of a dynamic Church whose life can vary in intensity. This means that the three marks of membership given by Pope Pius XII—namely, baptism, the faith, and union with the pope and bishops and the entire body of believers—can be present in the fullness attested to in the Scriptures or in lesser degrees.

Still another idea can be added which is not explicit in the encyclical but which does not contradict it, and which is made abundantly clear by the Second Vatican Council. We must say that the one-sided theory of membership only in the soul of the Church cannot be excluded; otherwise the resulting doctrine about the three marks of membership would likewise be one-sided. The three external conditions are to be understood as efficacious signs for participation in the salvation of Christ and in the Holy Spirit. The more intensely these three signs are realized by the individual, the more can he realize his participation in the salvation of Christ. The dynamic concept of the Church rests, therefore, on the understanding of the Church as a sacramental reality. If one sees the Church in its juridical aspect only, as is the case in the definition of Robert Bellarmine, then it is difficult to accept the idea of degrees of membership.

THE SECOND VATICAN COUNCIL

The Second Vatican Council devoted great attention and effort to this problem, essentially widening and deepening the scope of the question. Before this time only the Church membership of the individual non-Catholic Christian had come under consideration, but now Vatican II added to the first question a second which it considered of great moment, that of the ecclesiastical status of the non-Catholic Christian denominations. This question was not to be answered under the category of "membership."

"Full Incorporation" and a Dynamic Understanding of the Church

The Council distinguished between full membership in the Church and another kind of relationship which could not properly be called "full membership." Because of the exceptional ecumenical significance of the problem, the text (Constitution on the Church, #14) is quoted here verbatim:

> They are fully incorporated into the society of the Church who, possessing the Spirit of Christ, accept her entire system and all the means of salvation given to her, and through union with her visible structure are joined to Christ, who rules her through the Supreme Pontiff and the bishops. This joining is effected by the bonds of professed faith, of the sacraments, of ecclesiastical government, and of communion. He is not saved, however, who, though he is part of the body of the Church, does not persevere in charity. He remains indeed in the bosom of the Church, but, as it were, only in a "bodily" manner and not "in his heart." All the sons of the Church should remember that their exalted status is to be attributed not to their own merits but to the special grace of Christ. If they fail moreover to respond to that grace in thought, word, and deed, not only will they not be saved, but they will be the more severely judged.
>
> Catechumens who, moved by the Holy Spirit, seek with explicit intention to be incorporated into the Church are by that very intention joined to her. With love and solicitude Mother Church already embraces them as her own.

(See also the Decree on Ecumenism, #2.)

It is to be noted here that the idea of *votum* is applied only to the catechumens, of whom it is said that they are regarded by the Church as already belonging to her. For a correct understanding of the text it must be observed that the reference is to incorporation into the whole Church, not only the visible dimension. First of all, the threefold bond of Pius XII is mentioned—confession of faith, the sacraments, and recognition of Church authority. But this threefold bond would have no meaning for salvation if it did not at the same time effect union with Christ in the Holy Spirit. Referring to the sterility of a merely external membership in the Church, the Council emphasizes that full incorporation into the Church is not a static thing, but rather always in need of fulfillment. The incorporation, once done, must always be realized anew, and in the realization deepened. But this also means that the Church is always in the process of becoming more fully the Body of Christ and the People of Christ, the more its members give themselves in faith to Christ and his Spirit.

The Council, by the deliberate use of the expression "full incorporation" (*plena incorporatio*), leaves the way open for another kind of relationship. But to designate the relationship to the non-Catholic Christian communities the Council does not use the word "incorporation," but rather "association."

At the very beginning of the Constitution (#8) the way is prepared for a new view. Speaking of the uniqueness of the Church, the Council does not say simply that the one Church willed by Christ is identical with the Church governed by the Roman Pontiff. Rather it says that the one Church of Jesus Christ has concrete form, in the churches governed by the bishops in union with the pope (*subsistit in ecclesia catholica, a successore Petri et Episcopis in una communione gubernata*).

*Ecclesial Elements outside the Structure
of the Catholic Church*

The Council adds immediately that "many elements of sanctification and of truth, as gifts properly belonging to the Church of Christ, can be found outside the visible structure of the Catholic Church." This short comment is further clarified in the following text (Constitution on the Church, #15):

The Church recognizes that in many ways she is linked with those who, being baptized, are honored with the name of Christian, though they do not profess the faith in its entirety, or do not preserve unity of communion with the successor of Peter. For there are many who honor sacred Scripture, taking it as a norm of belief and of action, and who show a true religious zeal. They lovingly believe in God the Father Almighty and in Christ, Son of God and Savior. They are consecrated by baptism, through which they are united with Christ. They also recognize and receive other sacraments within their own Churches or ecclesial communities. Many of them rejoice in the episcopate, celebrate the Holy Eucharist, and cultivate devotion toward the Virgin Mother of God. They also share with us in prayer and other spiritual benefits.

Likewise, we can say that in some real way they are joined with us in the Holy Spirit, for to them also He gives His gifts and graces, and is thereby operative among them with His sanctifying power. Some indeed He has strengthened to the extent of the shedding of their blood. In all of Christ's disciples the Spirit arouses the desire to be peacefully united in the manner determined by Christ, as one flock under one shepherd, and He prompts them to pursue this goal. Mother Church never ceases to pray, hope, and work that they gain this blessing. She exhorts her sons to purify and renew themselves so that the sign of Christ may shine more brightly over the face of the Church.

The Decree on Ecumenism (#3) has the following important passages:

One cannot impute the sin of separation to those who at present are born into these Communities and are instilled therein with Christ's faith. The Catholic Church accepts them with respect and affection as brothers. For men who believe in Christ and have been properly baptized are brought into a certain, though imperfect, communion with the Catholic Church. Undoubtedly, the differences that exist in varying degrees between them and the Catholic Church—whether in doctrine and sometimes in discipline, or concerning the structure of the Church—do indeed create many and sometimes serious obstacles to full ecclesiastical communion. These the ecumenical movement is striving to overcome. Nevertheless, all those justified by faith through baptism are incorporated into Christ. They therefore have a right to be honored by the title of Christian, and are properly regarded as brothers in the Lord by the sons of the Catholic Church.

Moreover some, even very many, of the most significant elements or endowments which together go to build up and give life to the Church herself can exist outside the visible boundaries of the Catholic Church: the written word of God; the life of grace; faith, hope, and charity, along with other interior gifts of the Holy Spirit and visible elements. All of these, which come from Christ and lead back to Him, belong by right to the one Church of Christ.

The brethren divided from us also carry out many of the sacred actions of the Christian religion. Undoubtedly, in ways that vary according to the condition of each Church or Community, these actions can truly engender a life of grace, and can be rightly described as capable of providing access to the community of salvation.

It follows that these separated Churches and Communities, though we believe they suffer from defects already mentioned, have by no means been deprived of significance and importance in the mystery of salvation. For the Spirit of Christ has not refrained from using them as means of salvation which derive their efficacy from the very fullness of grace and truth entrusted to the Catholic Church.

The Council makes a distinction, in the Decree on Ecumenism, between the Eastern Churches, on the one hand, and the separated Churches and Communities in the West on the other. With regard to the first it says (#14):

It is worthy of note that from their very origins the Churches of the East have had a treasury from which the Church of the West has amply drawn for its liturgy, spiritual tradition, and jurisprudence. Nor must we underestimate the fact that basic dogmas of the Christian faith concerning the Trinity and God's Word made flesh of the Virgin Mary were defined in Ecumenical Councils held in the East. To preserve this faith, these Churches have suffered much, and still do so.

However, the heritage handed down by the apostles was received in different forms and ways, so that from the very beginnings of the Church it has had a varied development in various places, thanks to a similar variety of natural gifts and conditions of life. Added to external causes, and to mutual failures in understanding and charity, all these circumstances set the stage for separations.

(#15). Everybody also knows with what love the Eastern Christians enact the sacred liturgy, especially the celebration of the Eucharist, which is the source of the Church's life and the pledge of future glory. In this celebration the faithful, united with their bishop and endowed with an outpouring of the Holy Spirit, gain access to God the Father through the Son, the Word made flesh, who suffered and was glorified. And so, made "partakers of the divine nature" (2 Pet. 1,4), they enter into communion with the most holy Trinity. Hence, through the celebration of the Eucharist of the Lord in each of these Churches, the Church of God is built up and grows in stature, while through the rite of concelebration their bond with one another is made manifest.

In this liturgical worship, the Christians of the East pay high tribute, in very beautiful hymns, to Mary ever Virgin, whom the Ecumenical Synod of Ephesus solemnly proclaimed to be God's most holy Mother so that, in accord with the Scriptures, Christ may be truly and properly acknowledged as Son of God and Son of Man. They also give homage to the saints, including Fathers of the universal Church.

Although these Churches are separated from us, they possess true sacraments, above all—by apostolic succession—the priesthood and the Eucharist, whereby they are still joined to us in a very close relationship. Therefore, given suitable circumstances and the approval of Church authority, some worship in common is not merely possible but is recommended.

(#16). From the earliest times, moreover, the Eastern Churches followed their own disciplines, sanctioned by the holy Fathers, by Synods, even ecumenical Councils. Far from being an obstacle to the Church's unity, such diversity of customs and observances only adds to her comeliness, and contributes greatly to carrying out her mission, as has already been recalled. To remove any shadow of doubt, then, this sacred Synod solemnly declares that the Churches of the East, while keeping in mind the necessary unity of the whole Church, have the power to govern themselves according to their own disciplines, since these are better suited to the temperament of their faithful and better adapted to foster the good of souls.

(#17). . . . In the investigation of revealed truth, East and West have used different methods and approaches in understanding and proclaiming divine things. It is hardly surprising, then, if sometimes one tradition has come nearer than the other to an apt appreciation of certain aspects of a revealed mystery, or has expressed them in a clearer manner. As a result, these various theological formulations are often to be considered as complementary rather than conflicting. With regard to the authentic theological traditions of the Orientals, we must recognize that they are admirably rooted in holy Scripture, fostered and given expression in liturgical life, and nourished by the living tradition of the apostles and by the writings of the Fathers and spiritual authors of the East; they are directed toward a right ordering of life, indeed, toward a full contemplation of Christian truth.

Concerning the relationship toward the separated Churches and ecclesial communities in the West, the following texts from the Decree on Ecumenism should be noted:

(#19). . . . one should recognize that between these Churches and Communities on the one hand, and the Catholic Church on the other, there are very weighty differences not only of a historical, sociological, psychological, and cultural nature, but especially in the interpretation of revealed truth. That ecumenical dialogue may be more easily undertaken, despite these differences, we desire to propose in what follows some considerations which can and ought to serve as a basis and motivation for such dialogue.

(#20). Our thoughts are concerned first of all with those Christians who openly confess Jesus Christ as God and Lord and as the sole Mediator between God and man unto the glory of the one God, Father, Son, and Holy Spirit. We are indeed aware that among them views are held considerably different from the doctrine of the Catholic Church even concerning Christ, God's Word made flesh, and the work of redemption, and thus concerning the mystery and ministry of the Church and the role of Mary in the work of salvation. But we rejoice to see our separated brethren looking to Christ as the source and center of ecclesiastical communion. . . .

(#21). A love, veneration, and near cult of the sacred Scriptures lead our brethren to a constant and expert study of the sacred text. For the gospel "is the power of God unto salvation to everyone who believes, to Jew first and then to Greek" (Rom. 1,16).

Calling upon the Holy Spirit, they seek in these sacred Scriptures God as He speaks to them in Christ, the One whom the prophets foretold, God's Word made flesh for us. In the Scriptures they contemplate the life of Christ, as well as the teachings and the actions of the Divine Master on behalf of men's salvation, in particular the mysteries of His death and resurrection.

But when Christians separated from us affirm the divine authority of the sacred Books, they think differently from us—different ones in different ways—about the relationship between the Scriptures and the

Church. In the Church, according to Catholic belief, an authentic teaching office plays a special role in the explanation and proclamation of the written word of God.

(#22). By the sacrament of baptism, whenever it is properly conferred in the way the Lord determined, and received with the appropriate dispositions of soul, a man becomes truly incorporated into the crucified and glorified Christ and is reborn to a sharing of the divine life, as the apostle says, "For you were buried together with him in Baptism, and in him also rose again through faith in the working of God who raised him from the dead" (Col. 2,12; cf. Rom. 6,4).

Baptism, therefore, constitutes a sacramental bond of unity linking all who have been reborn by means of it. But baptism, of itself, is only a beginning, a point of departure, for it is wholly directed toward the acquiring of fullness of life in Christ. Baptism is thus oriented toward a complete profession of faith, a complete incorporation into the system of salvation such as Christ Himself willed it to be, and finally, toward a complete participation in Eucharistic communion.

The ecclesial Communities separated from us lack that fullness of unity with us which should flow from baptism, and we believe that especially because of the lack of the sacrament of orders they have not preserved the genuine and total reality of the Eucharistic mystery. Nevertheless, when they commemorate the Lord's death and resurrection in the Holy Supper, they profess that it signifies life in communion with Christ and they await His coming in glory. For these reasons, dialogue should be undertaken concerning the true meaning of the Lord's Supper, the other sacraments, and the Church's worship and ministry.

(#23). The Christian way of life of these brethren is nourished by faith in Christ. It is strengthened by the grace of baptism and the hearing of God's Word. This way of life expresses itself in private prayer, in meditation on the Bible, in Christian family life, and in services of worship offered by Communities assembled to praise God. Furthermore, their worship sometimes displays notable features of an ancient, common liturgy.

"Church" and "Ecclesial Communities"

It is to be noted in these texts that the word "church" and the word "ecclesial community" are used of the non-Catholic Christian societies without explicit clarification. In earlier ecclesiastical documents the word "church" was used only of the Orthodox, and this use in the years before the Council was very infrequent. When the Council thus uses the word "church" of non-Catholic Christian groups, there is ground for seeing that in the groups there are significant ecclesial elements, and when the distinction is made between church and community, it points significantly to the fact that in some denominations the ecclesial elements are negligible, while in other groups—for example, in German Lutheranism or in many groups in America—they are so numerous and so strong that the word "church" is appropriate. It must not be overlooked, however, that the word "church" is understood here in an analogous sense. E. Schlink says on this point: "It is not exactly stated which non-Roman churches are designated as churches and which as ecclesial communities, and in what dogmatic ecclesiological sense this concept is applied. But it is clear that the concept of a church community no longer represents a mere sociological characteristic, but is used rather of elements of Church existing in non-Roman Christianity. The traditional distinction of schismatic and heretical is lacking in the Decrees as well as in the Schema. It can be replaced by the ideas of church and ecclesial community."[1]

The Council repeatedly emphasized the union of non-Catholic Christian Churches and Church communities with the Catholic Church and the incorporation in Christ. At the same time it stressed that this association is not a full incorporation in the Church. As a norm for the distinction between "association" and "incorporation" it gives those same three signs which express full membership in the Church—namely, faith, the sacraments, and union with the successor of the apostle Peter and the other bishops. These three marks are not all lacking in the non-Catholic Christian Churches and communities. They have baptism together with faith in Jesus Christ as Son of God and Savior, which of course is the central reality of the Christian faith.

The Decree on Ecumenism also brings out that although the understanding of Christ as the Son of God and of his saving

---

[1] "Das Ergebnis des konziliaren Ringens um den Oekomenismus der romisch-katholischen Kirke," in *Kerygma und Dogma*, II (1965), 183f.

100 The Structure of the Church

activity, and also of justification, by the non-Catholic Christians especially, very often differs from the understanding of the Catholic Church, nevertheless they do share in common the faith-statements expressed in the ancient Church councils.[2] In this connection A. Grillmeier has rightly remarked that the formulations of the Decree on Ecumenism recall the formulas of the Ecumenical Council of Churches, which in New Delhi in 1961 adopted the following text: "The Ecumenical Council of Churches is an association of churches which confess the Lord Jesus Christ according to the Holy Scripture as God and Savior and strive together to accomplish that to which they are called, to the glory of God, of the Father, of the Son and of the Holy Spirit."[3]

It is natural that the Council should make a distinction between the Eastern and Western Christian denominations. The three characteristics essential for a "church" are present and realized to a certain degree in all Church communities. The element of church government also is to be found in Western, Protestant Churches and Church communities, for wherever there is a society, organization is needed. The question is only whether the government, and therefore the bishop's office, is regarded as a human or, as in the Catholic and Orthodox Churches, a divine institution, and whether or not it is connected with the idea of succession.

"Full Membership" and Christian Community

In view of the stress laid in the Constitution on the sacramentality of the whole Church (the Church is an original sacrament of the second order, as Christ is the original sacrament of the first order), it must be added to the above comments that "full membership" in the Church is not exhausted in the affirmation of the three salvific signs, but that it also means the possession of the Holy Spirit and his gifts, the interior life of faith and love, and that loyalty to Christ which can drive men to martyrdom and the

[2]Article on the Vatican Council in *LTK*, I (1966), 200ff.
[3]*Documentarbericht,* ed. W. A. Visser-t'Hooft (Stuttgart, 1962), p. 457.

witness of blood for him. It is in these inner elements of "full membership" that there is deep community.

There was no formal exposition of the status of non-Catholic Christian Churches and communities given by the Council, but in the sense of the Council the following can be said: Incorporation through baptism into the Church as a community in doctrine, in sacramental life, and in government by Peter's successor and the bishops guarantees participation in the death and resurrection of Jesus Christ. It is incorporation in the Church insofar as it is the Body and Christ is the Head. It effects a participation in the Holy Spirit, who is its life principle. Baptism has a powerful dynamism. It is ordered toward the celebration of the Eucharist, toward that central feast of the People of God in which they gather as brothers around their Lord, to eat his body and drink his blood. Through this action the believers in Christ become in a full and real sense and in an ever deepening way the Body of Christ. Whoever does not take part in the eucharistic celebration remains outside complete communion. He does not take part fully in the community, and, so to speak, remains in the vestibule.

It can be said: To the extent to which the three signs of full membership, especially participation in the eucharistic meal, are realized in living faith, in that measure does man grow in the mystery of salvation of Jesus Christ in the Holy Spirit. Whenever the Constitution speaks simply of the Church of Jesus Christ, it is this living, full realization which it has in mind. On the basis of experience, however, it also reckons with the possibility of a purely external affirmation of the three signs of membership without an interior participation. In this case the Church membership remains ineffective for salvation (Constitution on the Church, #14; Decree on Ecumenism, #4), since the fullness of membership which embraces both exterior and interior is lacking. Such a man does not cease to be a member of the Church, because he assents to the three external conditions of membership; but his membership has no saving significance for him, it only increases his responsibility.

The statements of the Council concerning the non-Catholic Christian Churches make clear that the three constitutive signs are not lacking in them; they are realized in the individual non-Catholic Churches in different degrees, but in none are they found in their fullness.

Ecumenical Progress

The Council treats in a positive way the elements which form a church. This fact distinguishes the Second Vatican Council from earlier ones, whose statements emphasized the differences, while the common elements were overlooked or minimized. Realistically, Vatican II neither failed to recognize the differences nor attempted to conceal them, but it rightly stressed the commonalities in the Christian faith—that is, the common ecclesial elements. These marks have the power to establish union with the Holy Spirit and with Jesus Christ present in the Holy Spirit, and to effect salvation. The Council appreciated the fact that the signs, though only partial, might be realized with such an intensity of faith and love that the Catholic Church would be able to see therein an ideal example (e.g., Decree on Ecumenism, #4). The Council pointed to the liturgical rites of worship and the Christian spirituality which have the power, even outside the Catholic Church, to issue in the giving of one's life for Jesus Christ. The Council rightly calls attention to this true fruit of the Holy Spirit in the non-Catholic Christian Churches, but at the same time it stresses that this situation in no way justifies the separation itself, and that the Catholic Church, together with all others, in obedience to Jesus Christ who willed only one Church, must exert every effort toward reuniting. In this connection it should be pointed out that this council no longer, as in earlier decrees, speaks of a "return," but rather of a reunion. This requires that all the Churches concern themselves to deepen their Christian understanding and to realize their Christian faith in brotherly love.

When the Council says that the Catholic Church feels herself obliged to let the marks of Jesus Christ shine forth ever more brightly in her whole exterior appearance, it is proclaiming publicly a commitment to a continuing inner reform, not to any exterior demonstration. The marks of Christ meant here are the sign of brotherly love. It is not true to say that there is an opposition here between the Protestant idea of hiddenness and the Catholic idea of display or pomp. Times without number in the Decree, the Council pointed out that the Church wants to give up every display of pomp, that she wills to go the way of poverty and self-denial with Christ (e.g., #7 or #8) and to engage in a constant self-reformation. The Church feels herself obliged to live that love which reached its highest and archetypal intensity in the self-surrender of Christ on the cross. What is spoken of is nothing other than the following of Christ. That it is a question of this following and not of some moralizing posture, again can be grasped only in faith. So we have here, joined in a happy synthesis, the Protestant principle of hiddenness, which is to say of the reality of Jesus Christ as comprehensible only in faith, and the Catholic principle of visibility, insofar as this is not a visibility proper to material things but one possible and understandable only in faith. Faith is the common, binding element.

Insofar as the marks of salvation are realized in the non-Catholic Christian Churches with particular dynamism, a reunion of the Churches could bring about a greater fullness and richness in the actualization of the Christian faith. Those elements which play a special role in these Churches could be strengthened in the Catholic Church. If, for instance, the Russian Orthodox or the Scandinavian Lutheran Church were to be united again with the Catholic Church, characteristics could come into play which are different from those of the Latin and Anglo-Saxon Churches. And so there would come about a more dynamic realization, not only of the uniqueness, but also of the catholicity of the Church.

For although the Catholic Church has been endowed with all divinely revealed truth and with all means of grace, her members fail to live by them with all the fervor they should. As a result, the radiance of the Church's face shines less brightly in the eyes of our separated brethren and of the world at large, and the growth of God's kingdom is retarded. Every Catholic must therefore aim at Christian perfection (cf. Jas. 1,4; Rom. 12,1–2) and, each according to his station, play his part so that the Church, which bears in her body the humility and dying of Jesus (cf. 2 Cor. 4,10; Phil. 2,5–8), may daily be more purified and renewed, against the day when Christ will present her to Himself in all her glory, without spot or wrinkle (cf. Eph. 5,27).

On the other hand, Catholics must joyfully acknowledge and esteem the truly Christian endowments from our common heritage which are to be found among our separated brethren. It is right and salutary to recognize the riches of Christ and virtuous works in the lives of others who are bearing witness to Christ, sometimes even to the shedding of their blood. For God is always wonderful in his works and worthy of admiration.

Nor should we forget that whatever is wrought by the grace of the Holy Spirit in the hearts of our separated brethren can contribute to our own edification. Whatever is truly Christian never conflicts with the genuine interests of the faith; indeed, it can always result in a more ample realization of the very mystery of Christ and the Church.

Nevertheless, the divisions among Christians prevent the Church from effecting the fullness of catholicity proper to her in those of her sons who, though joined to her by baptism, are yet separated from full communion with her. Furthermore, the Church herself finds it more difficult to express in actual life her full catholicity in all its aspects. (Decree on Ecumenism, #4)

◂ 11

The Unity of the Church's Life

The uniqueness of the Church is guaranteed through the unity of its life. This must not, of course, be understood as uniformity. There must be in the Church a certain pluralism, even on the basis of the fullness of revelation and its realization, but also because of the diversity of individuals and nations. This pluralism, however, cannot become so strong that it destroys unity and leads to a breakdown into individual groups. The Church will always be characterized by this tension between community and individuality. A formula without this necessary tension cannot be found.

UNITY AS GIFT AND AS DUTY

The unity in the life of the Church is as much a gift as it is a duty; first of all a gift from God, then the response in faith from man. The deepest ground for this unity is Jesus Christ present in her and the Holy Spirit sent from him, the life principle of the Church. The presence of Jesus Christ in the Holy Spirit realizes and manifests itself in many ways, but especially in the Eucharist, in which the People of God come as the body of Christ and *become* that Body. Here the communal life nourishes itself as a life in faith, hope, and love. The visible guarantors of the unity are the hierarchy—the pope and the college of bishops for the whole Church, the individual bishop in the diocese, the pastor in the parish. It is in this structure that the unity in multiplicity appears.

Christ and the Spirit as Basis for Unity

In the farewell speech of Jesus we see his overriding concern that the new messianic community of salvation formed around him be one. This is not self-evident, the less so since this community was formed with members of the Old Testament People of God, men who had not yet attained God's revelation.

The type of unity about which Jesus is concerned has its prototype and is rooted in that unity which binds him to the Father. It is precisely in this unity that the new community can be recognized as coming from God (Jn. 17,20–23). Christ points out that the unity cannot be created through human striving, but that once it is given, man carries the responsibility for it. It is of such importance that the continued existence of the Church is assured only so long as she is united in herself (Mt. 12,25; cf. Jn. 10, 11–16; 11,52). When Christ speaks of the unity of the Church as founded in the trinitarian divine life, he reveals at the same time how far it is from his intention to equate unity with uniformity. The one God exists only in the living interaction of the three divine persons. The tripersonal God can be understood only as the relation of the persons in the unity of the divine essence and as unity in the Father, who is the source without beginning of the other persons. The unity consists only in the threeness of the unmistakably distinct persons, as, vice-versa, the persons can exist only in the unity of the divine essence and in their origin from the Father.

The presence of the Son sent by the Father into the world (which sending has its end in the Church) and the abiding presence of the Holy Spirit form the inner, spiritual, foundation of the Church's unity. The faithful have only one Lord and one God. They have only one mediator (1 Tim. 2,5). They are brethren in the Spirit (1 Cor. 12; 10,17; 2 Cor. 5,14f.; 11,2; Rom. 3,29f.; 5,12.15–19; 7,4f.; 10,12). The unity dwelling in God himself expresses itself in the unity in the Church. In Jesus Christ all the faithful are, as it were, a single man (Eph. 2,13–22; 1 Cor.

12,13; Gal. 3,27f.; Col. 3,10f.). According to Paul, the baptized form, as it were, one person (Eph. 2,13–22). In First Corinthians he says (10,17) that the unity is created and ensured not only through the eating of the one bread but also through the power of the Spirit. But this does not mean a double principle of unity. In Paul's conception the glorified Christ, identical with the historical Jesus, is *the* principle. In baptism and in the Eucharist man is incorporated in Christ in still another way. Something of this kind is possible because in the resurrection Jesus assumed a spiritual existence, and as the spiritual existence and as the spiritual Christ, he can enter into man and receive man into himself. The Holy Spirit is the source of the spiritual life of Christ. In baptism and the Eucharist he unites man with the Lord-become-spirit. The letter to the Galatians (3,26–28) says: "For through faith you are all sons of God in union with Christ Jesus. Baptized into union with him, you have all put on Christ as a garment. There is no such thing as Jew and Greek, slave and freeman, male and female; for you are all one person in Christ Jesus."

The Christian concept of unity, based in the spiritual community of the Church, is distinguished from political conceptions. The Eastern peoples experienced unity in their monarchy, which they took for the expression of divine right. Alexander and Augustus attempted to realize the idea of a political world unity. When this disintegrated, there still arose a unity of culture. When today the Church also proclaims the cultural and political unity of all men, she sees the real possibility of this anchored in an ultimately spiritual depth. The love which is at work in the One Church should stretch out beyond the Church and embrace all men in a realistic but complete brotherhood.

The Hierarchical Structure as Guarantee of Unity

Just as the eucharistic eating of the one bread causes the many to be one body, and so the eucharistic celebration is the Church presenting herself as the one body of Christ, so the hierarchical structure forms the visible guarantee of the unity of the Church. Paul himself was the guardian of the unity of the local church in

Corinth against forces threatening separation. How important unity was to Paul is shown in the frequent and emphatic warnings which he sends to the churches he established. So, for example, in 1 Corinthians he says (1,10): "I appeal to you, my brothers, in the name of our Lord Jesus Christ: agree among yourselves, and avoid divisions; be firmly joined in unity of mind and thought." Love must, according to Paul, be the support of all in the Church, as living men are to the body of Christ (1 Cor. 13). The Acts of the Apostles also testifies to the manner in which the first believers cultivated and watched over the gift of unity (cf. Acts 1,11–14; 2,42–47; 4,32).

Unity in the Theology of the Fathers

In the age of the Fathers the "apostolic heritage" was seldom spoken of without emphasis being put on the idea of unity. In the rule of faith—the creed—especially, and in the celebration of the Lord's Supper, the expression and the guarantee of this unity was seen. According to the teaching of Ignatius of Antioch, Irenaeus of Lyons, Cyprian, and Augustine, unity was what distinguished the true Church from the pseudo-churches. The word "brotherhood" arises frequently in this context. Clement of Alexandria says: "For this reason we call them brothers, because they are born again through the very same Word" (*Stromata*, II,9). Tertullian (*Apologetic*, 39) justifies speaking of Christians as brothers by observing that we acknowledge one Father, have drunk one spirit of holiness, have been borne out of one womb into the light of truth and brotherhood.

So it is understandable that the Church focuses on unity as a central element of her self-understanding. This holds true, for example, of the exposition of the First Vatican Council (DS 3050ff.) and the ecclesiological statements of Leo XIII (DS 3291).

FAITH, HOPE, AND LOVE AS FORMS OF UNITY

Thomas Aquinas sees the perfect form of unity in the common faith, hope, and love of all the members of the Church (*On the*

Apostolic Confession of Faith, Art. 9). Faith is to be understood as *fides qua* as well as *fides quae*—that is, both as the subjective act of faith and its objective content. However, the unity of faith cannot be maintained in its proper sense unless the proclamation by the Church, through the Church's teaching office, is recognized as the formal principle of faith. On the basis of this formal principle, the unity in faith is maintained even when the believers do not embrace, acknowledge, and understand all of faith's content in the same depth and clearness. Unity is also preserved when there is readiness to accept what the Church puts forward for belief even when the content itself is not made explicit but is only a matter of implicit belief, or when special emphasis is given to particular ideas.

On the other hand, disagreement concerning the formal principle of faith is the deepest ground for general disunity, and this last would remain even if, by some happy coincidence, a broad unanimity concerning the objective content of faith should prevail. Division in faith cannot really be healed unless the Church is acknowledged as the interpreter and guardian of revelation.

As regards objective content, a basic element in the unity of faith is the recognition of the sacraments, especially baptism, and the living of the sacramental life. According to the Scriptures, baptism brings men directly into the community. Those who have received baptism belong together in a different way from those who live without it. This thesis retains its validity even though far-reaching differences of opinion exist among the baptized concerning the content of faith and the visible appearance of the Church.

Concerning hope, which Aquinas calls the second bond of unity, it should be observed that all the members of the Church form one pilgrim Church moving toward one future desired by all, toward the final, absolute future which is to be the perfection of the cosmos and the fulfillment of the history of man. In this world of hopelessness it is precisely this hope in the future which should always be witnessed to by the Christian believer. It is a testimony to the resurrected Lord who has already anticipated the future and opened it up for all others. Christians should not be deterred from this hope because of their experience that the calamitous forces of death, illness, strife, are still at work. In their hope they see a future in which these forces inimical to men are annihilated once and for all, having been fundamentally deprived of their power after the death of Christ.

It is love which is the most intense bond of unity and the bond of peace among men. Love finds its realization not only in the historical-ethical realm but sacramentally, in the Eucharist. Love is so important for the accomplishment of this central liturgical solemnity that Paul in his first letter to the Corinthians (11,23) can say pointblank that the celebration in Corinth does not deserve the name "Lord's Supper" because the rich Corinthians show an antisocial disposition during it. The failure in love is a mockery of the feast as well as of community. We can understand that it was very difficult for the rich Christians in Corinth, in high social positions, to sit down at table with workers and slaves, with Christians from the lowest rungs of the social ladder. But this is exactly what is required if the feast is to achieve its real meaning. What is done in the liturgy must then be proved in daily life (cf. 1 Cor. 13). Here it is to be noted that the praying and believing community expressing itself in the liturgy assumes the form of a suffering community, as in the celebration of the Eucharist the Church participates in a special way in the cross of the Lord. She enters into the suffering of the crucified Christ, so that with him she may come to the Father.

The sacramental participation in the cross of the Lord takes harsh and rigorous shape in the crosses of everyday life. Suffering becomes a sign of union with Christ; those who suffer, living memorials to him (Gal. 2,19; 6,17; 2 Cor. 4,10f.; 12,10; Phil. 1,29). So Paul can write (2 Cor. 4,11f.): "Thus death is at work in us, and life in you." To the Colossians he says (1,24): "It is now my happiness to suffer for you. This is my way of helping to complete, in my poor human flesh, the full tale of Christ's afflictions still to be endured, for the sake of his body, which is the church." This subject will be further considered in Volume V under the sacramentality of the Church.

UNITY AND MULTIPLICITY

In conclusion it should be stressed again that according to the whole witness of Scripture and tradition and of the Church's teaching, the unity of the Church is far from being a collectivity. The unity represents a community in which everyone not only preserves his own selfhood but also has the power to bring it to maturity. According to Paul, within the Church community each should bear the burden of the other (Gal. 6,2). Each one should examine his own conduct so that he is not a burden to others (6,4f.). The condemnation of party spirit is not a condemnation of individuality. Although truth and community, on the one hand, and freedom and autonomy, on the other, stand in a polarity, with the accent falling sometimes more on community, sometimes more on the individual, neither one of the elements can grow too rapidly without destroying the whole delicate balance of unity. Freedom is as primary as community. It does not rest on concessions, but rather has the same basis as unity; that is, the life of the baptized in Christ. It must impose only those limits on itself, or submit to the limits imposed on it, which are necessary for the well-ordered life of the community. Such a self-restriction on freedom has its ground in the love of the brethren. Freedom is the mother of plurality in the Church.

Multiformity has its basis in natural factors, namely in the characteristics of the individual members, in their membership in natural groups, such as a particular nation, family, or race; but it is also based supernaturally, in the inexhaustible fullness of divine revelation. In the Church we are dealing not merely with individual men with their different talents, viewpoints, inclinations, backgrounds, temperaments, but also with nations and their different characters. None of these should be destroyed; rather, every one should work itself out and be represented in the ordering of the whole. In this sense one can speak of the Church in France, in Italy, in Germany, in America, etc. It is always the same Church, but in its actual manifestation it bears the impress of the special characteristics of the land, the people, and their history. It is here that the richness of its life is revealed. It would only endanger unity if one man or people or one historical epoch had to be the norm for the whole.

Another ground for multiformity lies in the grace-filled nature of the Church herself. According to God's plan, the members of the Church have different spiritual gifts and commissions (cf. 1 Cor. 12). Natural and supernatural are often joined in this diversity of gifts. This holds true, for example, of the different theological schools, which answer controversial theological questions in different ways, out of different philosophical and experiential orientations. It is also seen in the different religious orders and associations in the Church.

◄ 12

Clergy and Laity in the One People of God

Here we must call to mind something that was said earlier about the Church as the People of God. In order to understand correctly the structure of the Church with respect to laity and clergy, we must keep in mind the unity of the Church and the community of all those belonging to it. The baptized form one People which exists as the Body of Christ and as the temple of the Holy Spirit. Within this People is a structure, based on directions given by Christ himself but assuming different forms at different times in the course of history. The structure of the Church includes a "lay state" and a "clerical state."

This twofold division is not affected by the fact of a "religious state"; the latter exists as a charismatic rather than a structural element in the Church, as a way of special fulfillment of the Christian life. The Second Vatican Council took this into account when it declared (Constitution on the Church, #43): "From the point of view of the divine and hierarchical structure of the Church, the religious state of life is not an intermediate one between the clerical and lay states. Rather, the faithful of Christ are called by God from both these latter states of life so that they may enjoy this particular gift in the life of the Church and thus each in his own way can forward the saving mission of the Church."

The distinction between clergy and laity is essential for an understanding of the People of God. These two states establish the structure of the Church; there is no other structural element. What are sometimes designated as such (e.g., the charismatic elements) are to be categorized as contributing to the perfection of life in the Church. As opposed to what separates those within the Church—the commonality—from the non-members, the differentiation of the charismatics is secondary. The difference between clergy and laity derives from the fact that different tasks are entrusted to them, and as a result they bear a different impress through baptism, confirmation, and ordination. The laity have, in common with the clergy, all the rights and duties which result from their primary status as members. In relation to salvation, the laity are on the same level as the clergy through faith and baptism. Through baptism a man becomes a member of the People of God. The differentiation within this community created by baptism also comes about through a sacramental process, through the sacrament of Orders in its several degrees, from its highest form in the consecration of the bishop down to the ordination of priests and deacons. Those who receive Orders do not lose all that they have in common with the rest of the Church, but a modification occurs, so that a new structural position and a new ministry arises. This new type of position and office means that the cleric is capable of fulfilling tasks which the non-cleric cannot do, and, on the other hand, that the cleric is not called and is not qualified to carry out in the same manner as the non-cleric all of the tasks to which the whole People are obliged; for example, the direct forming of the world and secular culture in the spirit of Jesus Christ. The clerics constitute the hierarchical organization in the Church and this is twofold: (1) There is a sacred hierarchy, which embraces the episcopacy, the priesthood, the diaconate, and the lower sacred orders. (2) There is also a jurisdictional hierarchy which includes the papacy and the episcopacy. Other offices are derived from these (the college of cardinals, the patriarchs, metropolitans, apostolic vicars, etc.). The twofold hierarchy corresponds to the distinction between the power of orders and the power of jurisdiction (K. Mörsdorf).

Rightly understood, this description of the Church's structure should do away with the concept of the Church as, above all, the pope and bishops' Church. The Church is neither the laity's nor the bishops'. It is one hierarchically ordered community of salvation in which every member has his own position and is called to fulfill duties proper to it. No one is a purely passive member. The call to action in the Church and the responsibility of all has already been brought out in the encyclicals *Mystici Corporis* and *Mediator Dei* of Pope Pius XII.

Just as in the natural body there is no such thing as a passive member, but rather every member has a proper function to carry out for the good of the whole, so it is true in an analogous way of the members of the Church, of the body of Christ. There is no distinction in this concept between the laity on the one hand and bishops and priests on the other. What appears here is the totality of God's People and the common status of all members. This commonality consists in the relation to Christ, in the resemblance to him, and in the participation in the Holy Spirit. God's saving intention is turned first of all to the whole, as we hear countless times in Holy Scripture. The subject of salvation is first of all the community, and the individual wins his salvation as a member of the community.

Since the People of God is the body of Christ and a people in Christ, all its members are destined to grow into the image of the Son, so that he may be the firstborn among many brethren (Rom. 8,29). They are united through baptism to the Lord who died on the cross and was glorified in the resurrection, and they are made like to him not so much in his being as in his saving activity. This likeness is eternally lasting. By the breaking of the eucharistic bread they share in the body of the Lord and become that body in which they are bound together with him and with each other into a community. All the members of the body must be formed in his likeness, until Christ takes shape in them (cf. Gal. 4,19). For this reason we are admitted into the mystery of his earthly life; we are made like to him, die with him and arise with him, until finally we rule with him (cf. Phil. 3,21; 2 Tim. 2,11; Eph. 2,6; Col. 2,12; etc.). The forming into Christ accomplished through baptism and the

Eucharist, and ever deepened, has far-reaching consequences for the members of the Church, for by this means they are enabled and obliged to cooperate actively in the mission of Jesus Christ.

We can place Jesus' mission in the context of a long tradition, since it contains elements of the mission of the prophet, of the priest, and of the king (the shepherd of his people). Every member of the people of God has a part in this threefold mission of Jesus. In the Church there is only the one priesthood, the one teaching office, the one pastoral office of the Lord himself, since Christ endowed the Church with his own mission. All its members take part in this one mission, some as laity, some as clerics. "The apostolate of the laity is a participation in the saving mission of the Church itself" (Constitution on the Church, #33). The Council's decree on the Laity stresses the diversity of the service and the unity of the mission. The most significant expression of this is the teaching about the independence of the laity within the organization of the whole. Its priestly, prophetic, and kingly dignity is not an attenuated participation in the office of the hierarchy; the laity are not an extension of the arm of the bishop. The full extent of the bishops' power belongs to the bishops properly as successors of the apostles and as a direct result of this succession, and they take part in the ministry of Christ in one way, through the commission to the apostles. The laity have another mode of participation, not derived from the bishops' but rather from the mission of Christ bestowed on the People of God. Insofar as the laity have a contribution to make to the mission of the whole Church, they have an official function in the Church (cf. Decree on the Apostolate of the Laity, #2 and #5). To the hierarchy there belongs, in addition, a new type of participation in the three offices of Jesus Christ. In a certain way this grows out of the participation common to all, but as the Council has emphasized, in such a way that it is not merely an intensification but actually a new kind of participation. It is a difference not only of degree but of kind.

The Second Vatican Council tried to find a formulation which would express the commonality and yet avoid the possible misunderstanding inherent in the expressions "special" and "general" priesthood, which had formerly been used. It spoke of a "common" participation in the mission of Jesus Christ proper to the family of God's People and of a ministerial commission deriving from the hierarchical office.

In a short glance back over history, it is to be noted that at the time of the Reformation no distinction was made between the different types of participation in Jesus' priesthood or in the rest of his mission. The idea developed by the Reformers, after similar theses had already been set forth in the teachings of Wyclif and Hus, was that all the baptized possessed a common priesthood, and that there was no other over and above this. But for the sake of the organization which is necessary in every community, one of the members of the group was chosen community leader. This process was called "ordination." Luther himself appears to have seen this procedure only as an emergency measure for the time when abuses were prevalent in the Church. However, what was originally understood to be an emergency measure and carried out as such remained through the centuries and became entrenched.

In the Catholic Church, in opposition to the theses of the Reformers, the hierarchical priesthood was specially stressed and the priesthood common to all was gradually forgotten. This development was disastrous, for it produced within the Church an unnecessary tension which found expression in the terms "clericalism" and "laicism." The relation between laity and priests appeared to be exhausted by command on the one hand and obedience on the other.

In our times, as a result of the new self-understanding on the part of the Church which has matured through the various crises of growth, the notion of the common priesthood again appears much stronger in the Catholic consciousness—that of the priest as well as of the rest of the faithful. But it must at once be added that we would be interpreting too narrowly if we were to ascribe to the hierarchy a participation only in the priestly activity of Jesus. For they have also a share in the prophetic and pastoral activity of the Lord. The Second Vatican Council spoke in detail about this threefold participation, but at the same time it taught, with an unmistakable concern, the difference between the common and the hierarchical priesthood. The subject of the laity is

treated in both the Constitution on the Church and the Decree on
the Apostolate of the Laity, as well as in almost all the other
constitutions and decrees, either explicitly or implicitly. It becomes very clear: the layman is the norm in the Church.

Also in the context of structural differences, there is within the
Church a most complex classification, not according to "states"
but on the basis of diverse apostolates to which individuals may
be called by the Holy Spirit. With reference to the Pauline image
of the body of Christ, the Second Vatican Council says (Constitution on the Church, #7):

As all the members of the human body, though they are many, form one
body, so also are the faithful in Christ (cf. 1 Cor. 12,12). Also, in the
building up of Christ's body there is a flourishing variety of members and
functions. There is only one Spirit who, according to his own richness
and the needs of the ministries, distributes His different gifts for the
welfare of the Church (cf. 1 Cor. 12, 1–11). Among these gifts stands out
the grace given to the apostles. To their authority, the Spirit Himself
subjected even those who were endowed with charisms (cf. 1 Cor. 14)
Giving the body unity through Himself and through His power and
through the internal cohesion of its members, this same Spirit produces
and urges love among the believers. Consequently, if one member
suffers anything, all the members suffer it too, and if one member is
honored, all the members rejoice together (cf. 1 Cor. 12,26).

The common element, therefore, according to the Council, is
more important than the differences. It extends beyond and
encompasses all the individual appearances and different groups.
It represents an effective *a priori* for all the individual manifestations, whether of laity or of priests. The differences within the
whole, it is true, are essential; but, in contrast with the primary
and fundamental distinction between Church members and non-
members, they are of secondary importance. The fourth chapter
of the Constitution on the Church (#32) notes:

Therefore the chosen People of God is one: "one Lord, one faith, one
baptism" (Eph. 4,5). As members, they share a common dignity from
their rebirth in Christ. They have the same filial grace and the same

vocation to perfection. They possess in common one salvation, one hope, and one undivided charity. Hence, there is in Christ and in the Church no inequality on the basis of race or nationality, social condition or sex, because "there is neither Jew nor Greek; there is neither slave nor freeman; there is neither male nor female. For you are all 'one' in Christ Jesus" (Gal. 3,28).

◂13

The Laity

WHO ARE THE LAITY?

The Second Vatican Council did not intend to give a definition of the laity. It particularly did not want to interpret the relation between the baptized living in the world and those living in a religious order or community without priestly ordination. It was content to propose a linguistic distinction. It explained (Constitution on the Church, #31) that the faithful who are not members of the priestly state or of an established religious order—i.e., the baptized who participate in the priestly, prophetic, and pastoral office in their own way and carry out their own part of the mission of the whole Christian people—should be called the laity.

It should be remarked that this description of the laity has nothing to do with the ordinary usage of layman as nonexpert. In the Church's language the word "lay" is intended to signify a particular status and mission within the whole body of the People of God.

When the Council speaks of the "state" of the laity, the word is not meant in any technical sense. The laity do not form a college which is placed over against the college of bishops. Nor is the word meant in any sociological-juridical sense. It expresses a negative aspect: non-clerical; and a positive one: participants in the priestly, prophetic, and pastoral office of Jesus Christ. For laity and clergy the same call to salvation and to holiness is the action of the Holy Spirit, who moves all interiorly to this end, that they love God with their whole heart, with their whole soul, with their whole mind and all their strength, and love one another as Christ loved his own.

THE RESPONSIBILITIES OF THE LAITY

The Council explains (Constitution on the Church, #30):

Pastors also know that they themselves were not meant by Christ to shoulder alone the entire saving mission of the Church toward the world. On the contrary, they understand that it is their noble duty so to shepherd the faithful and recognize their services and charismatic gifts that all according to their proper roles may cooperate in this common undertaking with one heart. For we must all "practice the truth in love, and so grow up in all things in him who is the head, Christ. For from him the whole body (being closely joined and knit together through every joint of the system according to the functioning in due measure of each single part) derives its increase to the building up of itself in love (Eph. 4,15–16)."

The laity therefore make their contribution toward the attainment of the universal, final, historical, cosmic end which Christ had in view in the building up of his Body, the Church (H. Schlier). The mission in the Church is in principle the same for all, namely to extend the message of Jesus Christ, to advance the kingdom of God.

If therefore everyone in the Church does not proceed by the same path, nevertheless all are called to sanctity and have received an equal privilege of faith through the justice of God (cf. 2 Pet. 1,1). And if by the will of Christ some are made teachers, dispensers of mysteries, and shepherds on behalf of others, yet all share a true equality with regard to the dignity and to the activity common to all the faithful for the building up of the Body of Christ. For the distinction which the Lord made between sacred ministers and the rest of the People of God entails a unifying purpose, since pastors and the other faithful are bound to each other by a mutual need. Pastors of the Church, following the example of the Lord, should minister to one another and to the other faithful. The faithful in their turn should enthusiastically lend their cooperative assistance to their pastors and teachers. Thus in their diversity all bear witness to the admirable unity of the Body of Christ. This very diversity of graces, ministries, and works gathers the children of God into one, because "all these things are the work of one and the same Spirit" (1 Cor. 12,11).

Therefore, by divine condescension the laity have Christ for their brother who, though He is the Lord of all, came not to be served but to serve (cf. Mt. 20,28). They also have for their brothers those in the sacred ministry who by teaching, by sanctifying, and by ruling with the authority of Christ so feed the family of God that the new commandment of charity may be fulfilled by all. St. Augustine puts this very beautifully when he says: "What I am for you terrifies me; what I am with you consoles me. For you I am a bishop; but with you I am a Christian. The former is a title of duty; the latter, one of grace. The former is a danger; the latter, salvation" (*Sermons*, 340, 1). (Constitution on the Church, #32)

The Council devotes special attention in its exposition to women. It does not consider them laity of lesser rank. The pastoral constitution, The Church within the Modern World, also emphasizes the responsibility and mission which are laid upon youth within the Church.

THE MISSION OF THE LAITY

While the Council stresses a threefold participation of the laity in the mission of Jesus Christ, it offers no systematic exposition of this. It does emphasize, however, that their mission is to be fulfilled both in the Church—that is, in the fulfillment of the Church's life—and in the world—that is, in collaboration with secular structures (Decree on the Apostolate of the Laity, #2).

The activity of the laity within the Church includes both liturgical and extraliturgical areas.

Participation in the Liturgy

The central act by which the laity partake in the priestly character of the universal Church is their participation in the commemoration of the death and resurrection of Jesus Christ. What the

Church is, she brings about over and over again in the eucharistic celebration. This is the feast of faith, in which the People of God presents itself as those belonging to Christ in faith, the family gathered around him. At the same time, through the eating of his body and blood in faith, the bond uniting the Christian to Christ in surrender to him grows deeper and more living. What takes place in the Eucharist is done by all together, although all do not participate in the same way. The Council assigns to the ordained priest as leader of the Eucharist a special role proper only to him, namely, to say the words of consecration, but it explains that all the People "cooperate" in the process. This cooperation, though difficult to interpret theologically, is a reality of great import. The Council explains, in agreement with statements of Pius XI and Piux XII, that those present offer the Lord Jesus to the Father, but that in addition all present, in and with the offering of Jesus Christ, make an offering of themselves. It can be said, in the spirit of Augustine, that the death and resurrection of Jesus and the glorified Lord himself are made present, so that those celebrating enter into his presence in the action of the offering; and thus, through him in the Holy Spirit, they are enabled to come to the Father. This presumes that they are giving themselves in charity to the Father and likewise to their brothers. The Eucharist implies right social behavior. It can be rightly celebrated only by those who make their whole life an offering to God for the brethren (cf. Acts 2,42–47; Rom. 12,1; 1 Pet. 3,15). It is in this sense that Paul's statement is to be understood, that uncharitable behavior destroys the meaning of the Lord's Supper—that it is, in fact, a mockery of community (1 Cor. 11,22ff.). The laity play a special liturgical role in the sacrament of matrimony.

All other worship of God grows out of the Eucharist, as from the center of the Church's life. It nourishes what the Decree on the Apostolate of the Laity calls the "witness of life," and the witness of the word. In answer to the question, What Church functions are reserved to the bishop and the priest? it must be said, strictly speaking, Only the presiding at the Eucharist, the giving of absolution in the sacrament of penance, and the conferring of holy orders. It would lead to a submergence once more of the laity in the Church if all the functions which do not strictly require priestly ordination were to be taken over by the deacon, and the layman assigned to purely secular tasks.

Participation in the Prophetic Office of Christ

The Council, further, calls special attention (Constitution on the Church, #12, #35) to the fact that Jesus, the great Prophet, carries out his prophetic task not only through the hierarchy, who teach in his name and with his authority, but also through the laity. Participation in the prophetic office of Jesus Christ is seen by the Council in the witness to Christ through word and example. It explains:

For that very purpose He made them His witnesses and gave them understanding of the faith and the grace of speech (cf. Acts 2,17–18; Apoc. 19,10), so that the power of the gospel might shine forth in their daily social and family life.

They show themselves to be children of the promise, if, strong in faith and in hope, they make the most of the present time (cf. Eph. 5,16; Col. 4,5), and with patience await the glory that is to come (cf. Rom. 8,25). Let them not, then, hide this hope in the depths of their hearts, but even in the framework of secular life let them express it by a continual turning toward God and by wrestling "against the world-rulers of this darkness, against the spiritual forces of wickedness" (Eph. 6,12).

The Sacraments of the New Law, by which the life and the apostolate of the faithful are nourished, prefigure a new heaven and a new earth (cf. Apoc. 21,1). So too the laity go forth as powerful heralds of a faith in things to be hoped for (cf. Heb. 11,1) provided they steadfastly join to their profession of faith a life springing from faith. This evangelization, that is, this announcing of Christ by a living testimony as well as by the spoken word, takes on a specific quality and a special force in that it is carried out in the ordinary surroundings of the world.

Consequently, even when preoccupied with temporal cares, the laity can and must perform eminently valuable work on behalf of bringing the gospel to the world. Some of them do all they can to provide sacred services when sacred ministers are lacking or are blocked by a persecuting regime. Many devote themselves entirely to apostolic work. But all ought to cooperate in the spreading and intensifying of the kingdom of Christ in the world. Therefore, let the laity strive skillfully to acquire a more profound grasp of revealed truth, and insistently beg of God the gift of wisdom. (Constitution on the Church, #35).

With regard to the witness to Christ through the Word, Scripture testifies to the effectiveness of members of the community not ordained (cf. 1 Cor. 12–14, especially 14,26–40). The baptized exhibited a great activity in the proclamation of the gospel (Acts 8,1–4; 11,19–21). In the First Epistle of Peter (1 Pet. 3,1) it is expected of the women that by their holy way of life, seen in its Christian meaning, they will win over their pagan husbands to the Christian faith without the latter's having heard the gospel (cf. 1 Cor. 7,12–16). In the letter to the Hebrews it is presumed that everyone who has belonged to the Christian faith for a time will become a missionary, bringing that faith to others. According to 3 John 8 it is evident that every member of the community is obliged to be active in the service of truth. We are reminded by the Council of the speech which Peter delivered on the occasion of the first Pentecost (Acts 2,15–18): "Now is fulfilled what was spoken by the prophet Joel: 'In the last days this will happen; I will pour out upon everyone a portion of my spirit; and your sons and daughters shall prophesy; your young men shall see visions and your old men shall dream dreams. Yes, I will endue even my slaves, both men and women, with a portion of my spirit, and they shall prophesy.'" Paul reminds the Thessalonians: "Therefore hearten one another, fortify one another—as indeed you do" (1 Thess. 5,11).

The "witness of life" of the laity includes all areas—the family, profession, science, technology, culture, politics—insofar as mutual brotherly concern operates in all the dimensions of human life. So there is no cleavage possible between one's professional and one's full Christian life. The Decree on the Apostolate of the Laity mentions some specific gifts which must be operative in daily living; e.g., friendship, humanity, uprightness, sincerity, courage, initiative, spirituality.

This "witness of life" is effective in the first place for the peace of men with God and one another. But it also brings about the renewal of society in the sense of that "new creation" which begins in history and will reach fulfillment in the final coming of Christ. Thus this "witness of life" is eschatological. The witness of life and the witness of the word are closely, in fact inseparably, connected. If life were detached from the witness of the Word, then the latter would become an empty gesture. The Second Vatican Council brings out how Jesus Christ as high priest of the new covenant vivifies the laity in his Spirit and urges them on to every good and perfect work so that he can continue his witness and his service through them.

For besides intimately associating them with His life and His mission, Christ also gives them a share in His priestly function of offering spiritual worship for the glory of God and the salvation of men. For this reason the laity, dedicated to Christ and anointed by the Holy Spirit, are marvelously called and equipped to produce in themselves ever more abundant fruits of the Spirit. For all their works, prayers, and apostolic endeavors, their ordinary married and family life, their daily labor, their mental and physical relaxation, if carried out in the Spirit, and even the hardships of life, if patiently borne—all of these become spiritual sacrifices acceptable to God through Jesus Christ (cf. 1 Pet. 2,5). (Constitution on the Church, #34)

There is ample testimony in the post-apostolic times to the active participation of the laity in the building up of the Church. Perhaps the oldest sermon we have (the so-called *Second Letter of Clement*) comes from the hand of a layman. Justin tells of the missionary preaching of the laity (*Dialogue with Trypho*, 3). The Gnostic Celsus makes it a matter for reproach of the Christians that the workers display great activity in order to spread Christianity (Origen, *Against Celsus*, 3,55). The Church historian Eusebius reports that Origen, although he was not a priest, was invited by the bishops to teach openly in the Church and to explain the Scriptures (*Ecclesiastical History*, 6,10). In the third century preaching by the laity became less frequent and then stopped altogether, until it received a new impetus in the thirteenth century through the Franciscan movement.

According to Augustine, an exemplary life is a visible word of faith. By it the witness to Christ is effected in the form of a sign. By means of this visible word the whole People of God preaches to the whole People of God, and to those also who do not belong to the People of God. Through it, Christ himself becomes visible, as the One who has given himself to the utmost for the brethren and their salvation. This kind of witness can disturb sinners, scoffers, and cynics and awaken them from their indolence. It can encourage and console those who stumble, who doubt, or who are ready to give up.

The words of consolation, of enlightenment, of encouragement, which Christians give to one another, have their source in that solicitous love in which they are fraternally devoted to one another. They have that distinguishing mark which Paul describes in First Corinthians as true charity (1 Cor. 13). Witness to Jesus Christ can only be given by such men, who are ready to have a share in the cross of their Lord. The word of proclamation, accordingly, receives its force from the celebration of the death of Jesus in the Eucharist.

The Council did not fail to comment on those special, extra-structural gifts which the Holy Spirit gives to both clerics and laity in order to witness to Christ in special situations—namely, the gifts which Paul indicates in his First Epistle to the Corinthians and which have come to be called charisms. However, the Council also notes that although such prophetic gifts are always required in the Church if it is not to become sterile, it is always necessary to distinguish false prophets from the true prophets. In this matter of charisms there are two dangers: the destruction of order and the exaggeration of order. The first leads to chaos, the second to *rigor mortis.*

Yves Congar distinguishes three forms of participation in the prophetic office of Christ. The first is authoritative proclamation, which belongs properly to the bishops alone (*ex officio*). Priests can share in this office (pastors on the basis of their delegated office) and so can the laity, on the basis of a commission given to them by the bishops (canonical mission). What is at work here is not only a natural teaching charism but also, and primarily, a share in the prophetic service of Christ carried out in still another way by baptism, confirmation, and orders. The second form is the unofficial proclamation of exhortation, of example, of apostolic activity—all nourished by the power of faith and love of Christ and the brethren. (This is the layman's "thing"!) The third form is the scholarly exposition of revelation, or theology. The same basic preparation is required for priests and laymen engaged in theology, although there may be practical differences in the situations in which they work.[1]

The laity can make their contribution to the witness of the Church both as members of groups (associations) and as individuals. The Council assigned the laity a special missionary task in mission lands. The Decree on the Church's Missionary Activity (#26) states: "Therefore, all missionaries—priests, brothers, sis-

[1]Yves Congar, *Lay People in the Church*, rev. ed. (Westminster, Newman, 1965).

ters, and laymen—each according to his own state, need preparation and training if they are not to be found unequal to the demands of their future work." (See also #17.) The laity make the presence of the Church in such lands real. To this end they should remain active members in the different areas of industry and society and so foster relations between the Christian faith and the non-Christian religions.

The participation of the laity in the pastoral mission of Jesus is treated only briefly by the Second Vatican Council. The real worth of the things of the world is expressly recognized by the Council (Decree on the Apostolate of the Laity, #7) at the same time that it warns of worldliness and a false secularization. Participation in the pastoral office of Christ is expressed chiefly in the fact that the faithful are freed from the power of the world, transplanted into the freedom of the sons and daughters of God, so that they need have no fear in the face of death or of any other forces, but can live in peace and joy.

It is out of this freedom that the laity should contribute, with the responsibility and initiative corresponding to their specialized knowledge, to a truly human shaping of the world in accordance with today's scholarship and technological progress, and in such a way that the brotherhood of man may prevail in all the areas of human endeavor.

In the pastoral constitution, The Church in the Modern World, the Council outlines the missionary task and the authority of the layman in the world. According to this document all men should feel themselves responsible for overcoming the darkness and the burden of ignorance and should be concerned to achieve for themselves and make available for others a genuine understanding and penetrating knowledge of the world. In this sphere the priest, according to the Council, should work only to support the layman, whose primary responsibility it is.

The Council states that the restoration of a right social order requires the cooperation of all, that no Christian can excuse himself from this work. If it is true that the Church is not bound to any particular political, social, economic, or cultural order, it is also true that it cannot be indifferent to any of them. For in them God is honored or despised, and Christ also, who is the head of creation. The men who are involved in the secular order are the same men whom the Church has to lead to salvation. This means that the order of the world must be so formed and shaped that man is enabled to live humanly, that brotherly love, liberty, and responsibility can flourish, and the believer can be free to live out his life in Christian faith.

Such a possibility is attainable only when the social order is in some way, however remote, an expression of that solicitous love which found its full realization in Christ. The Council stresses that for the fulfillment of this world mission, the laity must have freedom, a venturesome joy, initiative, independence, a sense of responsibility, sincerity, a spirit of comradeship, and magnanimity. Here active rather than passive virtues are recommended, by means of which men will create a great social order through their daily living together.

The Church makes an important contribution to this task inasmuch as, through the word of its gospel and its sacraments, it frees men from such socially dangerous attitudes as pride, self-seeking, and tyranny.

Because of the complexities deriving from technology and science which have entered the circumstances of human life and affect life-attitudes, we must expect that men of the same Christian faith, of equal competence and good will, will come to different—even opposed—conclusions with regard to the possible solutions of the most varied problems of life. The Council does not and cannot provide a particular solution for every given problem. It states only that in such cases men should exert every effort to arrive at an understanding with one another, that in any case mutual charity should be preserved. The laity are often urged by the Council, as a part of their world-mission, to cooperate with all men—non-Christians and atheists included—to extend and strengthen the bonds between men, to share their bread with others, and to meet all with esteem and respect. Apparent opposition can prove a stimulus to deeper and more thorough understanding. The Council texts point out that in the fulfillment of this world-task, the laity are subject to no direction or formation by the clergy. Their freedom is emphasized, and the risk of false steps which goes with any activity is accepted. By utilizing the progress in scientific and technical research, for example, the laity can contribute, through their mission to the world, to the propagation of the gospel and the expression of Christian love.

COOPERATION OF LAITY AND CLERGY

A radical and far-reaching event took place for Catholic thought on the Church when the Council declared:

If therefore everyone in the Church does not proceed by the same path, nevertheless all are called to sanctity and have received an equal privilege of faith through the justice of God (cf. 2 Pet. 1,1). And if by the will of Christ some are made teachers, dispensers of mysteries, and shepherds on behalf of others, yet all share a true equality with regard to the dignity and to the activity common to all the faithful for the building up of the Body of Christ.

For the distinction which the Lord made between sacred ministers and the rest of the People of God entails a unifying purpose, since pastors and the other faithful are bound to each other by a mutual need. Pastors of the Church, following the example of the Lord, should minister to one another and to the other faithful. The faithful in their turn should enthusiastically lend their cooperative assistance to their pastors and teachers. . . .

Therefore, by divine condescension the laity have Christ for their brother who, though He is the Lord of all, came not to be served but to serve (cf. Mt. 20,28). They also have for their brothers those in the sacred ministry who by teaching, by sanctifying, and by ruling with the authority of Christ so feed the family of God that the new commandment of charity may be fulfilled by all. St. Augustine puts this very beautifully when he says (*Serm.*, 340,1): "What I am for you terrifies me; what I am with you consoles me. For you I am a bishop; but with you I am a Christian. The former is a title of duty; the latter, one of grace. The former is a danger; the latter, salvation." (Constitution on the Church, #32)

The following statement is also significant:

The laity have the right, as do all Christians, to receive in abundance from their sacred pastors the spiritual goods of the Church, especially the assistance of the Word of God and the sacraments. Every layman should openly reveal to them his needs and desires with that freedom and confidence which befits a son of God and a brother in Christ. An individual layman, by reason of the knowledge, competence, or outstanding ability which he may enjoy, is permitted and sometimes even obliged to express his opinion on things which concern the good of the Church. . . .

Let sacred pastors recognize and promote the dignity as well as the responsibility of the layman in the Church. Let them willingly make use of his prudent advice. Let them confidently assign duties to him in the service of the Church, allowing him freedom and room for action. Further, let them encourage the layman so that he may undertake tasks on his own initiative. Attentively in Christ, let them consider with fatherly love the projects, suggestions and desires proposed by the laity. Furthermore, let pastors respectfully acknowledge that just freedom which belongs to everyone in this earthly city. (Constitution on the Church, #37)

Such statements show that the hierarchical element in the Church is essentially not patriarchal. Fraternal behavior is urged, and a continuing dialogue is encouraged among clergy and laity, in order to open up fruitful possibilities for the spread of the gospel.

‹ 14

Hierarchy: The Apostolic Origins of the Structure of Authority

OFFICE AND SPIRIT

It was the intention and mission of Jesus to establish and promote the reign of God. This reign of God was to attain its final form at the return of the glorified Lord. The seeds of it were planted by Jesus in those acts by which he laid the foundation of the messianic community, the Church, which is both the sign of its beginning and the means of its realization. Jesus created the college of the Twelve as representatives of this new community (Mk. 3,14); however, it is the entire body of the messianic community which is of central importance. For even when the calling of the apostles is seen as forming the temporal beginning of the new community, the meaning of the apostolic college still rests in the fact that it is the core of the new messianic community, to be finally constituted a community by the Holy Spirit. The apostles are to represent the final community of God's salvation, and also, by proclaiming the message of salvation and by accepting those who, believing, receive the good news, extend the community to the ends of the earth and nurture it to the end of time (Mt. 28,18ff.): the eschatological community of salvation. When the risen Lord parted from the Twelve with this commission, and when he finally confirmed them as apostles by the

132

sending of the Spirit, then the question arose of the apostolic succession. Connected with this is another important problem, namely that of the authority of the new community.

Even on a purely natural basis it is evident that a community of men in a historical setting cannot exist without societal and legal elements, and the Church, of course, is of such a kind. However, it is a community of a unique type, and the core of its societal structure must derive from Jesus Christ.

We must now investigate the relationship between Jesus' actions during his life and the subsequent structure of the Church.

Toward the end of the last century the Protestant theologian Rudolf Sohm defended a widespread and longstanding thesis when he said that the true nature of the Church stands in direct contradiction to Law. He maintained that the charismatic form of the primitive Church, in which only the power of persons led by the Spirit prevailed, was transformed toward the turn of the first century into the "sacramental-legal" early Catholicism, and that toward the end of the twelfth century this form was further modified into the corporate-legal constitution of the new Catholic Church. That is, authority in the Church detached itself from "the sacred," from its sacramental roots, and became independent. No doubt the various offices in the Church could have developed in this way, but today this thesis is generally rejected even by Protestant theologians. Nevertheless there remains an observable difference between Catholic and Protestant interpretations of the structure of the Church. Luther distinguished between the invisible, spiritual Church and the empirical one, and, correspondingly, between a human and a divine law. Divine law has its place in the spiritual Church, in the Church of the saints. Its sphere of activity is the interior of man. In the domain of the visible, the human law of the Church is dominant. This is not to be understood as secular law in the sense of civil order, for it is a law of a unique kind. While the law proper to the spiritual Church has to do with the inner man—that is, with his salvation—the law proper to the visible Church is concerned with the outer man. It is not a primary obligation—that is, not for the sake of salvation—but a secondary obligation—that is, for the sake of order. Man submits to order not because of faith but out of love, since without order the Church cannot live and act.

For an understanding of Catholic ideas about the legal structure of the Church one must keep in mind its basic christocentric constitution. God has communicated himself to men in Jesus Christ irrevocably and finally. It is true that his self-communication is an invitation; yet it is not without binding force. It contains within it a summons, even an obligation. The acceptance of the divine invitation on the part of men is a decision about salvation. In this view the life and activity of Jesus himself already contains elements of law inasmuch as it includes the claim of God on men, even though it be a claim which brings about their salvation. The grace-filled presence of God in Jesus Christ becomes judgment for him who rejects the faith. The self-communication of God realized in Christ remains living and effective until the end of time. It has its concrete form in the Church—in its proclamation, its dispensing of the sacraments, its governance. The Church is the presence of the grace of God.

The Church is the community of those who, through faith and baptism, accept the offer of salvation in Christ, who receive it ever anew and transmit it to others through proclamation and witness. The association of Christ and those who believe in him with one another requires a corresponding structure, unless it is to be in an invisible, spiritual sphere where nothing is binding, like a kind of gnostic school. There is no order without law. Furthermore the extension, and even more the mediation, of the divine self-communication to others requires a particular order—an order founded on the divine commission. The preaching of those commissioned by Christ has the same character of obligation as his own.

We must take into account the origin of the Church through the sending of the Holy Spirit on the first Pentecost, and the decisions of the men inspired by him, as well as the subsequent historical development of the structure of the Church. Since, according to Scripture, Christ never spoke in clear terms of a particular mode of structure for the post-apostolic Church, but rather simply endowed it with certain legal elements, it is understandable that we encounter in apostolic times a long period of experimenting and searching, of grappling with the problem. There could scarcely be a church, for instance, without some distinction between laity and hierarchy. These legal elements are the product of an historical development, but they can also be seen as the expression of the divine will. It is certainly true that the structure of the Church is conditioned by contingent historical situations and reflects them. In the course of the centuries the Church has availed herself, in theory as well as practice, of legal ideas and language from the secular field, just as theology, the scholarly reflection upon divine revelation, has used ideas from philosophy and non-biblical realms. However, in this process the characteristic difference between church law and civil law has been maintained. The Church represents in its social constitution an effective sign of salvation, and so the law of the Church has the stamp of the holy upon it.

A Christian sees in the Church a divine law together with a human one. The line between cannot always be exactly drawn, even though, basically, the difference is always there. When it comes to the manner in which structural relationships are to be concretely realized, human factors, such as temperament and "milieu," play no insignificant role. The effort being made today, toward a decentralization of the papacy, is an example of this. The Church is likewise concerned today about a new form for her entire liturgical life. And this in turn has as a consequence that the office of bishop appears in a new light. We are aware of the numerous changes which have been undertaken in the course of the last few years in relation to canonical regulations and to the changing of canon law.

Where there is law, there are authority and obedience, superior and inferior. Law gives to the officials in the Church a spiritual authority. The power given through the law means an obligation of service, and the greater the power, the graver the obligation (Mt. 20,25ff.). The exercise of authority, therefore, is a service of brotherly love. There should be no opposition between law and love in the Church, between the official Church and the spiritual Church. The official Church is the very channel and instrument for the working of the Spirit. Yet the Spirit has not bound himself exclusively to the structure. He blows where he will (Jn. 3,8).

Those who hold office in the Church should be filled with the Spirit and led by him. We should be able to say that in the person of officials Jesus Christ himself is active in the Holy Spirit. Ecclesiastical office implies that there is finally in the Church only one authority, only one spiritual power, only one teacher, one mediator and one shepherd, Christ the Lord. So the idea of ecclesiastical office should not mean rigidity or ossification, but rather a freeing from human narrowness and self-will for the service of Jesus Christ. Ecclesiastical office should ensure the freedom of Christian men. It should serve to put Christ and the faithful in direct contact with one another. In a certain sense it should demythologize all holders of office, including the secular, in that it shows for what end they have their power, namely, in order to serve.

In actual history, of course, tensions between the hierarchy and laity have been many and various. A constant self-examination is required of all the members of the Church in this regard. The conflicts have their basis in human weakness and sinfulness, which can lead, on the one hand, to lust for power, and on the other, to authoritarianism or flattery. Thus we can understand the constant warnings which are given by the Second Vatican Council out of a tradition which goes back to the very early Church (Constitution on the Church, #27, #32, #37). In the First Epistle of Peter (5,1–5), for example, we read:

And now I appeal to the elders of your community, as a fellow-elder and a witness of Christ's sufferings, and also a partaker in the splendor that is to be revealed. Tend that flock of God whose shepherds you are, and do it, not under compulsion, but of your own free will, as God would have it; not for gain but out of sheer devotion; not tyrannizing over those who are allotted to your care, but setting an example to the flock. And then, when the Head Shepherd appears, you will receive for your own the unfading garland of glory. In the same way you younger men must be subordinate to your elders.

It was in much the same sense that Bernard of Clairvaux addressed his disciple, Pope Eugene III (*De Consideratione sui*, III, 6): "Above all, consider that the holy Roman Church, which directs you with divine power, is a mother and not a lord, so that you may be not the lord but the brother of the bishops, and one with them."

In the official Church, the personal element of the salvific encounter in faith and love is bound up with the institutional. The personal operates in the institutional framework, and should operate in this way, so that the work of salvation is not stifled by the forces of personalities and commands are not given out of the joy of commanding. It should not be forgotten that freedom always has priority, and there should be commands only insofar as these are necessary. However, is is only the eye illuminated by love which can recognize this. When love is alive in the institutional operation, it will not degenerate into a bureaucracy. The personal element in the official functioning—that is, the intention to minister—has its ultimate foundation in the Holy Spirit, or Christ, who works through the officials. The official takes the part of Christ in his official activity, so that in and through him Christ should be concretely present. This demands that he shall willingly become the instrument of Christ, the crucified and risen Lord. For the administration of the sacraments the minimum requirement is that the minister have the intention of making the usual sign of witness to Christ. The one in authority is therefore personally engaged in his ministry, not only inasmuch as the accomplishment of the salvific action depends on him but also in that his own salvation is involved. Were he not willing to bind himself to Christ, he would be guilty of an abuse of the institution whose minister he is, and so would be endangering his own salvation. The execution of office is, in its very meaning and essence, always a performance of faith and love.

There is no absolutely reliable preservative against the danger present in all law of rigidifying into bureaucracy. However, on the basis of what Christ promised about the action of the Holy Spirit in the apostles, we may hope that the Spirit will successfully preserve the Church against such dangers. This can happen in different ways: through the constantly renewed stirring of the spirit of Christ in the officials themselves, or through the calling of the laity to a greater love and understanding of Christ, to a heightened sense of responsibility and a spiritual courage which,

joined with an enlightened and sure conscience, make them able
to alert the hierarchy to the need for reform. This activity of the
Spirit aims at holiness—at holiness in the universal sense of that
genuine and true fraternal charity which is realized in the world
and turned toward the world. The words of St. Paul still hold
good: "I may speak in tongues of men or of angels, but if I am
without love, I am a sounding gong or a clanging cymbal" (1 Cor.
13,1). Love is the law and the measure of all commands and all
obedience. But love is the work of the Spirit. And the words of
the apostle are never to be forgotten: "Do not stifle the Spirit"
(1 Thess. 5,19).

THE APOSTOLIC SUCCESSION

The officials of the Church hold their office as successors of the
apostles. The problem of succession will be considered first in
general and then with regard to the individual Church offices. It is
very difficult, given the limitations of the available sources, to
describe with any accuracy the historical process by which the
threefold office of bishop, priest, and deacon developed at the end
of the apostolic age.

First of all, it must be stated that nowhere in Scripture do we
find any word of Christ instructing the apostles to appoint
successors, or to pass on their mission in the form of the
episcopal or priestly office. However, it seems implicit in the
nature of the apostles' commission that they should appoint
successors. For the gospel must be proclaimed to the end of time,
and there was no new channel set up for men to be given this
divine self-revelation. The eschatological character of revelation
requires a succession. The Church is essentially apostolic. There
is general agreement among Christian theologians on this point;
the differences in opinion lie in the explanation of that apostolicity. In any case, the Church is apostolic on the basis not only of
its origin but also of its teaching. The Church of Christ knows that
its teaching should be identical with the message announced by
the apostles. The Catholic Church, the Orthodox, and the Angli-
can all add succession in office as a third essential element of
apostolicity, very closely connected with the second. The apos-

tolicity of teaching, in this view, is based on succession in office, and the point of the apostolic succession lies in the unabridged and undistorted proclamation of the message of Jesus, in the passing on of the pure gospel.

When Protestant theologians deny the apostolic succession, the argument used is that the office of apostle was unique and therefore could not be handed down. This is correct, insofar as the apostles, in a strict sense, were eyewitnesses who could testify in their preaching to what they themselves had seen and heard. But they were the definitive bearers as well as receivers of the revelation. If the apostles have successors, these can never receive a new revelation. They cannot in any way be eye- or "ear"-witnesses. But the uniqueness of the apostles' situation does not exclude the continuance of their mission, that is, the preaching of the gospel until the end of time. When the risen Christ explains that in his apparent absence he will all the while remain present with them until the end of time (Mt. 28,20); when he gives them the command to carry the gospel to the ends of the earth (Acts 1,8); and especially when, after his ascension, he calls still another new apostle, Paul, and gives him a special, far-reaching mission; all of this points to the conviction of the early Church that Jesus' mission must be carried on after the death of the apostles.

Here it must be noted that these successors have no other task except to proclaim the message of the apostles, to interpret it and pass it on. In this sense it is correct to say that the apostles' mission of proclamation underwent a change of structure, although not a change of content, through the formulation of the canon, when the Sacred Scriptures were gathered into a collection which then became fixed and binding in faith. While the apostles could give witness on the basis of their experience of Christ and their enlightenment by the Holy Spirit, the later successors are bound to the canon. This is the norm for all the activity of the Church in post-apostolic times.

On the other hand, Scripture does not proclaim itself: it remains dumb except through the voice of living men. Jesus built his Church upon men, on the saving encounter of man with man (Rom. 10,14–18), and not upon a book, even though he did provide for the genesis of such a book. The proclamation is necessary for the sake of salvation, and salvation is brought about in the salvific encounter. The Church therefore has a structure based on persons rather than things, personal rather than material. But if the word "structure" is taken in its narrow sense, the personal can be understood only as "the institutionally personal," so to speak. This structure is of so unique a kind that we find no parallel for it outside the Church. It is one and the same Spirit who, in and through the Church, brings about the objectivizing of the salvific message in the written word, and who is active in the proclamation of this message in the objectified Scripture. However, the objectivized message of salvation becomes capable of being heard only through the word of the proclaimer. It was a conception born out of the spirit of humanism—that Renaissance movement wherein the ancient Greek and Latin literature became known to the West—which ascribed to Scripture itself the role of proclamation. The principle "Scripture alone," which is still found in the Protestant Church today, rests on such a humanistic misunderstanding.

So the question arises, Who gives voice to the dumb letters of Scripture, so that the word proclaimed by Christ and the apostles can be heard in every age? One could answer, Every Christian, insofar as every Christian is united with Christ through baptism and confirmation and is filled with the Holy Spirit. That is, in fact, the opinion of Protestant theology, nor is the idea rejected by the Catholic Church (cf. the discussion on the role the laity). According to Luther, Christians are, through baptism, bishops and priests. Similar views had already been put forward by the Englishman Wyclif and his disciple Hus. Luther built an organization around this concept. In the Lutheran Church there is a calling and an ordination by the community, acting in this instance through its representative. Those so appointed have the office of proclaiming the gospel and therefore possess a spiritual character. It is possible that Luther came to these conclusions because he believed that the Church officials of that time, namely the bishops, had refused the task of reform, and on these grounds he put the priestly office into the charge of every Christian. To the objection that the community is not capable of examining the

Christian teaching and rejecting a false preacher, Luther rejoined that the Holy Spirit is operative, so that what might happen if the community were left to itself would actually not happen—namely, the corruption of the teaching of Christ.

The only thesis which is consistent with the picture of apostolic times and the conviction of the early Church is that although everyone had to bear witness to Christ, the authentic or binding proclamation occurred only through those commissioned by Christ. These were first of all the apostles. The apostles in their turn soon appointed co-workers and helpers, who had many and various tasks. In the earliest time there was no single terminology agreed upon to designate these apostolic helpers and co-workers. This is not to be wondered at in the time of the emerging Church. Christ himself had, according to Luke (10, 1–20), gathered around him not only the Twelve, but also other disciples. The passage from Luke recalls an Old Testament scene (Num. 11, 16f.) where Moses, at the bidding of God, had to associate to himself seventy elders, that they might rule the People of God with him. They received of his spirit; that is, they shared in his authority.

Early in the apostolic age such co-workers were themselves called apostles; this is true in particular of Matthias, chosen at the suggestion of Peter to fill up the college of apostles after the desertion of Judas (Acts 1,15–26). Some of the early Christian missionaries also received this title—Barnabas (1 Cor. 9,5f.), Junias, Andronicus (Rom. 16,7), Apollos (1 Cor. 4,6.9). Probably this extended meaning of the word was first used in Antioch for the authorized missionaries who went out to preach Christ (Acts 13,2f.; 14,4). In the letter to the Hebrews (3,1), Christ himself is called apostle, insofar as he was the one sent, commissioned and authorized by God.

Before we speak of the co-workers of the apostles individually, a general observation must be made. The question is whether, in the conviction of the early Church, appointment of such co-workers was a purely human action or the result of a divine ordinance—in other words, whether it was human or divine law that was operative here. The question is all the more warranted because, to cite an example, Paul clearly distinguishes between his message given as an apostle appointed by Christ and those pronouncements which derive from his human concern, even though the latter are born of faith (1 Cor. 7,12.40). It is clear that by their appointment of co-workers the apostles considered that they were fulfilling the comission of Jesus Christ and that therefore this appointment was by divine ordinance. The text from Luke (10,2) would seem to show that it corresponded to the will of Christ that the apostles should appoint such co-workers. In any case they had a share in the divinely appointed missionary task of the apostle. Nor can one overlook the fact that the apostles in their turn must be thought of as bearers of revelation. The presbyters ("elders") appointed by them, who were apparently men of considerable reputation inasmuch as they shared in the labors of the apostles, shared also in the office of apostle. The apostles themselves are sometimes referred to as "elders" (Acts 11,30; 1 Pet. 5,1; 2 Jn. 1; 3 Jn. 1).

In Jerusalem the "elders" were usually named together with the apostles and associated with them as a council (Acts 11, 27–30). The so-called Council of Apostles, which made the decision about the mission to the Gentiles, was a gathering of apostles and presbyters, or elders (Acts 15,6). The apostles and the presbyters composed the Council's resolution, and together they made the decision to communicate this conclusion to Antioch. The letter directed there begins with the words: "We, the apostles and elders, send greetings as brothers to our brothers of gentile origin in Antioch, Syria, and Cilicia" (Acts 15,24). The wording of the text which follows, "It is the decision of the Holy Spirit and our decision," makes it evident that the elders are included in this "our" (Acts 15,22.23.28). The college of presbyters of the early Church in Jerusalem had as its model the Jewish council of elders consisting of seven respected men, who presided over the community of the synagogue. Jewish elders formed, together with priests and scribes, the Sanhedrin, the central governing board. It can be said that the word "presbyter" is the most ancient title for a co-worker of the apostles. Thus the form of the Jewish synagogue had an influence on the structure of the early Church. Only gradually did the messianic community cut itself off from Judaism as it developed other recognized forms and its own liturgical structure.

We see another situation in the Pauline communities outside Jerusalem. We may accept the fact that the apostle and the co-workers chosen by him—Philip, Timothy, Apollo, Titus, Silas, Sosthenes—attempted to found Christian communities after the fashion of wandering missionaries. Over these communities the apostle would place a leader, often with no definite title. The reality existed before the designation. Our information about these processes is extremely sparse. However, we can probably accept the description given in the *Chronicle* of Arbela and the *Ecclesiastical History* of Eusebius, tracing the development of the Christian community in general. What can be known about the Pauline communities we learn from the early epistles. We can see from the letter to the Romans (12,6-8) and from 1 Corinthians (12,28-30) that there were a variety of offices which were exercised by the faithful inspired by the Holy Spirit, without any official appointment having been made. Paul did not oppose this process. He only required a right ordering of charity in the community life. Besides those who spoke with tongues there is mention also of prophets, teachers, preachers, wonder-workers, administrators. The important thing is that all offices of this kind serve for the building up of the community, that all the members be one in faith, in hope and love. Paul himself exercised, from a distance, a growing authority. These varied offices were not all permanent. They were gradually reduced to a few minimal offices. Occasionally the presbyters are also called *episkopoi*. This word expresses their function as overseer and leader more precisely (Acts 20,28; Phil. 1,1).

THE OFFICE OF BISHOP

The Foundation in the Intention of Christ

On the presupposition that the bishops are the successors of the apostles, we put the explanation of the bishop's office under the heading of the apostolic mission and interpret it as the commission given by Christ to the apostles. If the apostles could not pass on to the bishops as their successors the fact of being eyewitnesses, they could nevertheless pass on all those elements of their apostleship which would guarantee the proclamation of the gospel and the continuance of the messianic, eschatological community.

Justification for the statement that the apostles appointed successors to themselves is seen by Vatican II (Constitution on the Church, #20) in the fact that they passed on to their immediate cooperators, as a kind of testament, the duty of perfecting and consolidating the work begun by themselves, and instructed them to entrust this same ministry to other approved men who would in turn carry on after them. The bishops participate in a special manner in the threefold office of Christ as teacher, priest, and pastor.

Among the various ministries which were exercised in the Church from the earliest times, the Council gives the chief place to the office of bishop in virtue of a succession going back to the very beginning.

The New Testament texts cited by the Council (Acts 6,2–6; 11,30; 13,1; 14,23; 20,17; 1 Thess. 5,12–13; Phil. 1,1; Col. 4,11; Acts 20,25–27; etc.) show the beginnings of that later development which we find in post-apostolic times. In the "Teaching of the Twelve Apostles" (*Didache*) there appear resident officials, chosen from the community itself, who are called "bishops" and "deacons."

The letter of Clement of Rome to the church at Corinth (*I Clement*) around the end of the first century (perhaps from the year 96) states that the presbyters, who evidently formed a council, were installed by the apostles in accordance with God's will, to insure that everything be done in order. The presbyters have the duties, now assigned to bishops, of supervision and guardianship (44,4). In fact they are actually called bishops. They receive their authority from God himself or from Christ (16,1f.). The church in Corinth to which the letter is written is still governed by a council of presbyter-bishops.

A generation later the Shepherd of Hermas shows us a similar picture in Rome. In the letter which we have from Polycarp to the church in Philippi, we see the writer as presbyter in the sense of the single bishop of Smyrna. The apostle John had appointed him as such. But in the church at Philippi there is still a council of presbyters, over which a "wandering apostle" has final supervision.

The seven letters of Ignatius of Antioch provide us with a detailed theology of the bishop's office. Apparently in the communities to which he writes there prevails the same jurisdictional situation as in Antioch: a single bishop at the head, with a council of presbyters as advisors and deacons. The letters are addressed to the Magnesians, the Philadelphians, the Ephesians, the Trallians, and the Smyrnians. The intention of Ignatius is the maintenance of unity. He sees unity assured through the bishop, around whom the presbyters and deacons gather. Since the bishop is the embodiment and guarantor of unity, nothing may be done in the community without him. In the person of the bishop the community presents itself as one, its communion rooted in Christ himself. The bishop is the center of love. He is the living, loving reflection of all the members of the community in the unity of the love of Christ. No Eucharist is lawful unless it is celebrated in the presence of the bishop or someone authorized by him. In the person of the bishop Polybius, who paid a visit to Smyrna, Ignatius saw the whole community of Tralles as if in a mirror. For him the bishop is the representative of the community. Finally, he interprets the office of bishop christologically: Christ acts in the bishop. It is an obvious conclusion when Ignatius declares that the bishop presides in the place of God. But his theology is somewhat unclear when he goes on to state that the presbyters preside in the place of the apostolic college. Ignatius evidently unites the sacramental and juridical elements, without, however, giving much weight to the latter.

Like Ignatius in the East, Irenaeus was the first in the West to use the designation "bishop" (*episcopus*) for the local resident leader of the community. He is also the first, together with Hegesippus, to speak explicitly of the apostolic succession. According to Irenaeus, every local church since the time of the apostles had a single person at its head. In every community, bishop followed bishop. It is true this cannot be proved for all the communities, but it suffices to establish proof for the most well-known of them, the Roman Church. The bishop is therefore not only the guarantor of unity in each generation of believers but also the surety for the tradition, the guarantee of continuity of each generation with the primitive Church. Such a man has claim to the title "elder," a word which expresses his loyalty to the tradition. The continuity is immediately apparent only in those sees which can be traced back directly to an apostle. But those bishops whose churches were founded from one of the apostolic churches also stand in a line of succession to the apostles. The line of succession is considered by Irenaeus and Hegesippus to be crucial, for this continuity establishes the unity and identity with the teaching of the apostles and with Jesus Christ himself. It is not sufficient that a bishop simply carry out the apostolic commission; he must also stand in the line of succession from the apostles. This is constitutive for the office of bishop, even though in most concrete instances the actual line of transmission is not historically demonstrable.

We can judge the importance which the ancient Church attached to this continuity of tradition from the lists of bishops which were later composed. Like Irenaeus, Hegesippus in the middle of the second century in Rome stated emphatically that he had satisfied himself in the course of his sojourn there that there had been an unbroken tradition in which the pure teaching had been continuously handed down from the apostles to his own time. The bearers and the guarantors of this teaching were the bishops.

The Power of Jurisdiction and the Power of Orders

For a right understanding of the office of bishop it is extremely important to distinguish the power of orders and the power of jurisdiction. The mission committed to the disciples by Christ encompassed a variety of powers—the mandate to preach, to baptize, to celebrate the Eucharist, to lead the community. But despite the diversity of functions, the authority of their mission was to be understood as single and undivided, bestowed by Christ or by God himself. But in the course of development within the

Church a separation of powers came about as follows: through the laying on of hands and prayer an appointed leader, the bishop, would be ordained for a particular community with the consent of that community. The laying on of hands signified always both the empowering and the commission to have charge of a particular church. A difficult question would arise if such a local bishop, through his mode of life or heretical views, should prove himself unworthy. He could no longer serve as bishop but would have to be removed from office. It became a question, then, whether, with the removal, he at the same time lost his spiritual power.

The Donatists in North Africa had so lofty a conception of the sanctity of the Church that they declared that only holy men could be the ministers of the Church's holy power. The sinner, by his sin, lost all his spiritual power, he could not administer the sacraments, celebrate the Eucharist, or forgive sins. Augustine played a decisive role in this debate. Although he did not himself find a satisfying solution, he did prepare the way for one by his teaching about the spiritual character, the mark of consecration which remained even with the heretical bishops. This, according to Augustine, it is not possible to lose. It represents in some way a likeness to Christ, who is the reason why such a bishop can administer the sacraments. It was through painful experience that the distinction was learned between the power of orders, which cannot be lost, and the power of jurisdiction, which can be. The greatness of the theological difficulty involved can be seen from a decree of the Council of Chalcedon, which ruled out as meaningless the idea of an absolute ordination, that is, an ordination by which the one consecrated would not at the same time be appointed bishop of a particular local church, because a man so ordained would not be able to exercise his power.

But although an understanding of this distinction between the power of orders and the power of jurisdiction is indispensable for a right ordering of the facts of Church history, it does contain within it an incipient danger—namely, the possibility that pastoral authority shall be considered merely an external addition and that only the power of orders shall be regarded as significant for salvation in the proper sense. In the Middle Ages the power of orders was associated with the eucharistic body of Jesus Christ, and the power of jurisdiction with the mystical body, the Church. This division, which was almost universally accepted by the theology of the post-Tridentine era, might cause us to overlook the fact that the two powers, originating in the same root of the one undivided mission of Christ, cannot be completely separated from each other. Their interrelation is such that there can be no consecrated (priestly) activity in which the power of jurisdiction is not involved, and conversely, no jurisdictional (administrative) action in which the power of orders does not play some part.

According to the ruling of the Church, the possession of the power of jurisdiction presupposes the power of orders. The two powers are so interlocked that episcopal consecration always confers a basic element of the power of jurisdiction, even though, as we have already seen, the legitimate exercising of that power is not a necessary concomitant.

The distinction of the two powers is not so much an objective one as a formal, functional one. The power of orders, as we have seen, cannot be lost or given up, while jurisdictional power can be lost by removal from office. The power of orders ministers to the divine life in men, creating, deepening, safeguarding it. The power of jurisdiction serves the salvific ordering of community life. The power of orders can be exercised throughout the entire Church; the power of jurisdiction is limited either to a region or to certain persons, since it is ordered only to those for whom the official is appointed.

About the end of the eighteenth and the beginning of the nineteenth century the question arose in Catholic theology—influenced to some extent by Protestant theology—whether to these two powers there should not be added a third, namely the power of teaching. The issue was raised in connection with the doctrine about the three offices of Christ and the consequent threefold commission of the Church to sanctify, to proclaim the gospel, and to govern. The theological discussion became extremely lively in the nineteenth century . Nevertheless the First Vatican Council retained the traditional twofold division, subsuming the authority to teach under the power of jurisdiction, without completely identifying the two. But it must be admitted that the way in which the three duties of the Church—to proclaim the gospel, to dispense the sacraments, and to govern—are to be associated with the two powers of the Church, and these in turn are to form a single, holy, basic authority or power, constitutes a difficult problem.

The duality of sacred powers, which in their origin represent only one power, plays a major part in the statements of the Church about the bishop's office, so much so that the passages are hardly understandable unless this duality is kept in mind. We see here the inclination to include the pastoral office in the sacramental sphere, in this way removing the danger of schism or rupture.

The Office of Bishop as a Participation in the Mission of Christ

There are certain elements which the Church has repeatedly emphasized in treating of the apostolic succession. As opposed to the Reformation doctrine of the single priesthood which belongs in the same way to all the baptized, the Council of Trent declares that besides the priesthood common to all there is also a special priesthood of the ministry. This is in effect to set up a hierarchy with the "special" priesthood embracing bishops, priests, and ministers, and with the bishops set over the priests and ministers (DS 1776). The First Vatican Council defined the primacy and gave it great prominence, but at the same time, in a brief passage, emphasized that the authority of the papacy worked no prejudice to the regular and direct power of the bishops. The first detailed presentation of the bishop's office in the Catholic Church was provided by the Second Vatican Council. The entire Constitution on the Church bears on this topic, especially Chapter III, together with the Decree on the Bishops' Pastoral Office. In its declaration the Council did not promulgate solemn definitions, but it did state as Catholic doctrine a number of theses which had been disputed till then, in particular the teaching on the college of bishops and on the sacramental character of the bishop's consecration.

To begin with, it is evident that the Council does not intend to make any exclusive case for the office of bishop, but rather wishes to bring out that among the different ministries which were practiced from earliest times in the Church, according to the testimony of tradition, the function of bishop occupies a most prominent place. This does not make the other offices in the Church unimportant; on the contrary, it underscores their significance. The bishops undertook, as it says, the service of the community together with assisting priests and deacons, and through their ministry Christ remained present actively in his People, in the People of his heavenly Father.

It is clearly the conviction of the Council that the bishop's office is divinely instituted, and that therefore the Church could never take on a non-episcopal form of organization. However, the way in which the establishment of the bishop's office can be traced back to the will of Jesus Christ is not very clearly explained by the Council. One could imagine an express directive of Jesus not reported for us in Scripture; or one could think of the founding of the bishop's office in the commission of Jesus to the apostles; or its origin could be conceived as necessarily contained within the very nature of the Church, or as a decision of the apostolic Church itself. This last appears to be the most sensible. The apostles were not only the receivers but also the bearers of revelation. The Council can apply to the bishops the word which Christ spoke to the apostles (Luke 10,16). Whoever hears them, hears Christ, and whoever despises them, despises Christ and him whom Christ sent.

The priesthood of the bishops is understood and described as a participation in the priesthood of Jesus Christ himself. It is included in the priesthood of Christ and makes it concretely manifest. In the bishops Jesus Christ is present in the midst of the faithful as high priest. It is he himself who through their ministry proclaims the word of God and dispenses the sacraments of faith; through the fatherly service of the bishops he perpetually brings new members into his body, the People of God, in virtue of their rebirth in the Spirit. Through the prudence and wisdom of the bishops he himself leads the people of the new covenant on the pilgrimage to their eternal home. The bishops are accordingly servants and instruments of Jesus Christ.

‹ 15

The Episcopal College: Collegiality; Relation to the Papacy; Mission of Proclamation

THE COLLEGE OF BISHOPS

The bishops form a college. The word "college," of course, is not to be understood technically; it means simply that they form a permanent community. This collegiality is founded in tradition, being prefigured in the collegiality of the apostles themselves. However, it was proclaimed as a distinct teaching for the first time by the Second Vatican Council. This pronouncement included the statement that collegiality has its roots in apostolic times, and like the apostolic succession itself, is a matter of divine law. The Council put great emphasis upon the doctrine of collegiality as the answer to problems left open by the First Vatican Council—namely, the question of the relationship of the bishops to the papacy and the directly related question of whether the papal authority does not undermine the authority of the bishops to the extent of reducing them to the status of servants of the pope. This latter idea was in fact occasionally expressed after the First Vatican Council, and it appeared to find a certain real justification in the subsequent historical development of the papacy. To avoid possible misunderstanding regard-

151

ing the pronouncements of the Second Vatican Council about the office of bishop and its collegial character, the theological commission of the Council provided an explanatory "preamble" which also treated of the papacy. It was published together with the decrees of the Council. From the closing address of the Pope on the day of promulgation of the Constitution on the Church, it is clear that the Council text must be understood in the light of this explanatory preface. The preface makes clear that the word "college" must be understood as a stable group of persons whose structure and authority are derived from the early Christian Church, and not simply from an analysis of the concept. For this reason, instead of the word "college," another word is occasionally used—for example, "order" or "body."

The statement, made for the first time by the Second Vatican Council, that the individual bishop's office is essentially related to the community of bishops (Constitution on the Church, #22) can be attributed to the growth in the Church's understanding of its faith: "Just as, by the Lord's will, St. Peter and the other apostles constituted one apostolic college, so in a similar way the Roman Pontiff as the successor of Peter, and the bishops as the successors of the apostles are joined together." The idea had been suggested at the First Vatican Council, although the Council itself issued no decree on the subject. The meaning of collegiality as taught by Vatican II is that the power of the episcopacy lies in the community of bishops rather than in the bishops as individuals. The individual bishop receives his authority through being accepted into the college of bishops. Since the college is both a sacramental and a hierarchical community, the sacramental foundation of each individual episcopate becomes clear.

The Council based its doctrine of collegiality chiefly on the fact that the bishops are the successors of the apostles and, like them, constitute a college. The college of bishops succeeded to the college of apostles. The individual bishop is a successor of the apostles insofar as he is a member of the college. In the college of bishops the college of apostles continues to exist and to operate until the end of time. From this fact there arises a very important consequence for our faith: if the college of bishops succeeds to the college of apostles, it has then the character of an institution founded in apostolic times, and so is an institution of original and basic importance for Christianity. In this connection it should be emphasized once more that the college of bishops did not, and could not, take over all the elements of the apostolic college, and that different interpretations are possible as to the manner in which the succession is revealed. The Council did not express an opinion on this, although it did propose the doctrine that the collegial character of the college of bishops corresponds to a divine ordinance. On this basis the episcopal college has an authority, a ministry, and a commission which do not result simply from adding together the powers and ministries of the individual bishops.

As the basis of its teaching on this matter, the Council points to the fact that since ancient times the bishops have been joined in community not only with one another but with Rome through the bond of unity, of love, and of peace; it further points to the councils which were held to arrive at a common solution of difficult and important matters. It refers also, even though only secondarily, to the tradition that a bishop is always consecrated by a number of other bishops acting together, never by one alone.

THE EPISCOPAL COLLEGE AND THE POPE

In opposition to the conciliar concept of the superiority of the council of bishops over the pope, which had held sway for several centuries before it was rejected by the First Vatican Council, the Second Vatican Council points out emphatically and in numerous texts that the pope, the bishop of Rome, belongs to the college of bishops and presides over it; this is so essential that without the pope there is no college of bishops; the college has spiritual authority only insofar as the bishop of Rome is a member and presides as its head. The membership of the pope as head is thus definitive for the college. Without his membership it would be only a gathering of individual bishops. An exceptional situation arises when a pope dies, or becomes unable to carry out his office as a result, for example, of mental illness or a lapse into heresy or schism. In such an exceptional case the college of bishops does not cease to be a college. It does not break up into a gathering of individual bishops, because important unifying factors remain operative, namely their unity in the confession of Christ, unity in the Spirit, in love, in the eucharistic celebration. These factors are effective and play a controlling role also in cases where the pope is presiding as head of the college. From this it becomes clear that the collegial unity does not have a merely external ground, but must be interpreted sacramentally. The pope is definitively significant for the college as the visible expression of a unity founded ultimately in the sacramental dimension. For the rest, the Church is obliged, in such an anomalous exceptional case, to restore the head, which it does by the election of a new pope.

The collegiality of the bishops presents a difficult theological problem in relation to papal authority. The First Vatican Council stated that the bishop of Rome, in virtue of his office as vicar of Christ and as shepherd of the whole Church, has full, supreme, and universal authority; that he has the power to exercise it always and everywhere, and does not need the consent of the bishops. To this thesis of the First Vatican Council, the Second Vatican Council added (Constitution on the Church, #22) that the college of bishops, or the episcopal order, acting together with the bishop of Rome as its head, likewise is the subject of the supreme and full power over the universal Church.

In this statement the Council asserted of the college of bishops what was already the general Church teaching respecting the general councils. Although the word "universal" is used in the statement on papal authority, while it is missing in the statement on the authority of the episcopal college, this does not actually signify any difference. Although it is obvious from the texts of the Council, still the explanatory preface, in order to anticipate any possible misunderstanding, stresses, in connection with the relationship between the Pope and the episcopal college (#3): "There is no distinction between the Roman Pontiff and the bishops taken collectively, but between the Roman Pontiff by himself and the Roman Pontiff together with the bishops. Since the Supreme Pontiff is the head of the college, he alone can perform certain acts which in no wise belong to the bishops, for example, convoking and directing the College, approving the norms of action, etc." It is significant that in the preface the point is explicitly made that the pope, at his discretion, can apply different methods depending on the requirements of the time, that he need not confine himself to a form chosen once for all times. It is up to the pope, to whom the care of the whole flock of Christ has been entrusted, to determine how that care can most feasibly be exercised in accordance with the changing needs of the Church. This decision can be either personal or collegial. Although it is not stated in the final text of the Council, nevertheless one may accept that the pope also acts as head of the college in those cases in which he exercises his authority by virtue of his own decisions, without the cooperation of the bishops and also without any incentive derived from them. For he always speaks not only in the name of the Church but also for the Church. When he acts as pope it is never as a private person but always as the successor of Peter on whom the task of bringing the tradition to fulfillment among the People of God devolves. The college of bishops possesses the supreme and full power not as a gift or concession from the pope, but in virtue of its own competence, as a result of the provision of Christ. But since the pope's membership is constitutive for the existence and operation of the college, the concurrence of the pope is required for every conclusion of the college; and, properly speaking, not as a confirmation following the action, but *a priori* as an element integral to the decision itself and forming it in the first place. This holds true even when the approval of the pope has the external form of a confirmation following the decree, as is evident from the formula with which the decisions of Vatican II were published.

The way in which the pope exercises his function as head and member of the episcopal college can be expressed differently (cf. the reference at the end of #22 in the Constitution on the Church). Here the historical situation is of great importance. The participation of the pope can range from a voluntary though tacit acceptance of the decision of the bishops to papal initiative and solemn proclamation. The pope himself makes the decision as to which form he chooses. On the basis of historical events, specifically the events of the early councils, the assumption is warranted that the way in which the pope exercises his right and power is determined by human-historical factors to such a large extent that the observer who is not judging from the viewpoint of faith is able to see in such events nothing but the human and historical.

The fact that, on the one hand, the college with the pope presiding and, on the other hand, the pope alone without the college possesses the supreme and full power in the Church leads to a question which seems to be unanswerable—in fact to what seems to be a contradiction. The question is whether in the Church there are not two concurrent supreme authorities, or whether the fact that the pope exercises supreme authority without the college does not deprive the college of its power. Theologians have given different answers to this question. The traditional answer says that it is a question of two different and incomplete instrumentalities of ecclesiastical supremacy, incomplete insofar as the pope himself belongs to the episcopal college. According to another theory there is only one proper subject of supreme Church authority, namely the college constituted under the pope. This thesis safeguards the primacy of the pope; its proponents add that with this definition as to where the supreme power lies, the distinction must be made between actions which the pope alone performs without the college, even though in the name of the college, and those which, with the authoritative participation of the pope, have a strong collegial character. From a strictly legal or logical point of view it would perhaps be more correct to call the pope the single agent of the supreme power and to add that he can exercise this power either alone or together with the bishops in a collegial act. The unity of the Church through the dynamism of the supreme power in it would appear to be assured by such a thesis. However, it is also assured by the acceptance of two different incomplete organs, since both are bound together into a unity by the fact that the pope is the head of the college, and so the power of the primacy suffers no loss or threat through this thesis. Probably the decision for either option in this case is to be made more on the basis of psychological or legal and logical considerations than on any theological grounds.

In any case it holds true that the pope cannot stand alone; his unity with the bishops is an essential element of Catholic structure. Even though it is not to be denied that he is always capable of exercising his power freely, nevertheless the responsibility he bears for the unity of the Church constantly refers him to the collegial union with the bishops. He has, precisely as do the college of bishops, the obligation to maintain and to be ruled by the Word of God as it is written or preserved by tradition. The activity of the Roman Pontiff must be directed to the welfare of the Church (Preface, #3).

For this reason not only the bishops but also the pope, using all the necessary means—especially with the help of theological scholarship—must be concerned to expound revelation properly and to present it appropriately. This concern comes within the sphere of the pope's power of jurisdiction. In order that it be exercised conformably to the will of Christ, it must, like the exercise of human freedom, adhere to the divinely established content, which means to what is found in Scripture. Since revelation is directed to man and would therefore remain meaningless if it were not to reach man, to proclaim the gospel rightly means to be concerned that men shall understand it, and not only in a general, theoretical manner, but concretely, in their contemporary, historical situation. So we find included among the means listed as suitable by the Council, the dialogue with the contemporary world to which the gospel is to be preached. This includes dialogue with the non-Catholic Christian Churches and with the great non-Christian religions as well; for these also can be a stimulus and contribute to a proper, or to a deeper and more comprehensive, understanding of divine revelation. The pope with his supreme authority is by no means excused from such dialogue. In fact, because of his position of supreme power he is all the more obliged to such effort. It would not be simply a moral failure but an offense against his very office if he were to give up the attempt.

These considerations of matters within the scope of our problem appear to include a great number of unsettled questions. One might ask: Could not the pope, without formally abolishing or excluding the episcopal college, nonetheless effectively deprive it of its power, even though in principle this would contradict his own prerogative of primacy? Viewed logically or theoretically, it seems that such a situation could occur; but the

Catholic believer is confident that it will not. The Holy Spirit will not abandon the Church. In this truth we have the guarantee that what might be a strictly logical possibility will not come to pass if it would damage or destroy the Church of Christ. The relation between pope and college of bishops is not finally reducible to a transparently clear and detailed juridical formula. And this is not be wondered at. It remains in the realm of mystery, in the realm of the Holy Spirit, in whom alone, and not in men, the Christian reposes his final hope.

THE EXERCISE OF COLLEGIALITY

The collegiality of the bishops can be exercised in numerous ways. We must speak of a collegial act in the strict sense in every case where the pronouncement of the bishops evidently expresses a viewpoint in which the total body concurs. A method of voting can be employed here. But then there arises a major difficulty. Can it be said of the result of a vote that it really expresses the will of the college, and not of only a part of the college? Is a two-thirds or a three-fourths majority sufficient, or is a unanimous vote necessary? There is no absolutely certain answer to this question. It must be left to the college itself to determine the conditions for voting which will result in a pronouncement that can be considered as a collegial action. In ordinary everyday usage we might say that a moral unity must prevail. There is no strictly juridical answer. One might go on to raise the related question whether it is possible at all to decide about a truth by voting. In the case of other disciplines, like natural science or philosophy, this is simply impossible. However, in the case of voting by the episcopal college, it is a question not merely of the determination of a truth, but of the confession of Jesus Christ. The vote has the meaning of a confession of faith.

The most certain instance of collegial action, of course, is to be found in the outcome of a council. Since this is true, one could ask whether councils should not be held at shorter intervals than they have been in the last few hundred years, so that the divine institution of episcopal collegiality can be operative. However, the exercise of collegiality is by no means limited to councils. The

Constitution on the Church points out that collegial unity also appears in other ways, namely in the reciprocal relations of individual bishops to the local churches as well as to the universal Church. Although each bishop has real authority only over that part of the People of God entrusted to him, and not over other churches nor over the entire Church, he must nevertheless be concerned for other churches and for the universal Church. It is the concern of all the bishops, for example, that the gospel shall be preached to the entire world. And as a corollary to this universal concern comes the injunction that local churches blessed with earthly goods should come to the aid of poorer churches.

Another specific question is whether the regular teaching office proper to all the bishops is to be considered as the exercise of collegiality. Formally, this does not seem to be a collegial act in the proper sense, since every bishop teaches as the individual shepherd of a local church. In practice, however, the conformity of the teaching as it is set forth in catechisms, in sermons and the like, amounts to the same thing as a collegial act. The express or tacit agreement of the pope is always presupposed. When the popes (Pius IX, Pius XII, for example), before defining certain doctrines, have questioned the bishops, the answer of all the bishops can be understood as a collegial act. By a decree of September 15, 1965 (*Apostolica Sollicitudo*), Pope Paul VI set up a synod of bishops. It is thought of as a standing council of bishops for the universal Church. Even though it has only an advisory function, it can be given an executive power by the pope. Only the pope can convoke it.

THE EPISCOPAL COLLEGE AS SYMBOL OF DIVERSITY AND UNIVERSALITY IN THE CHURCH

To treat, finally, of the sacramental dimension—that is, of the realm of the Holy Spirit as eternal presence of Christ—just as unity is made visible in the pope, so is diversity and universality made visible through the episcopal college. The individual bishop is, of course, the visible principle and foundation of unity in his own church, as Cyprian says: "The bishop is in the church and the church is in the bishop" (*Letters*, 66,8). The bishops are the representatives of the local churches which they guide. The totality of the local churches is not to be understood as a sum, the result of a process of addition. Rather, each church under the care of an individual bishop is a manifestation of the universal Church. This is true of every local church. We can say that the local church is representatively identical with the universal Church. Such an expression is justified by the doctrine we find in the Pauline epistles. Paul writes to the church in Corinth, or the church in Thessalonica or the church in Galatia. Each individual church represents the whole. Although this view has not been sufficiently stressed—in fact, it was for a long time forgotten—nevertheless it has never disappeared entirely from the consciousness of the faithful. The local churches are like members in which the whole is always present and operative. It is precisely in this characteristic that we find the expression of the diversity and variety, the plurality, of the one Church. What prevails in the one Church is not the uniformity of complete equality and likeness, but a pluralism and diversity which does not disintegrate into opposing elements even though the whole contains many tensions within itself. The pluralism also is the work of the Holy Spirit, who obviously desires not uniformity but diversity. This is visible in the many bishops, just as the unity of the sacramental foundation of the Church is visible in the pope. God is mirrored in the Church as One and also as Three.

ADMISSION INTO THE COLLEGE OF BISHOPS

How does a person become a member of the episcopal college? Vatican II gives the answer: through sacramental consecration and hierarchical communion with head and members of the college (Constitution on the Church, #22). Two elements are mentioned here as the basis of membership.

First of all, concerning the consecration, the Council expressly teaches, in contradistinction to the view of the Middle Ages and in conformity with the modern thesis, that the consecration of a bishop is a sacrament, that it in fact represents the highest form of priestly ordination. The fullness of the power of Orders is conferred through the bishop's consecration. The Council refers to the fact that in liturgical practice and in the language of the holy Fathers, episcopal consecration is called the high priest-hood, the epitome of the sacred ministry.

For from tradition, which is expressed especially in liturgical rites and in the practice of the Church both of the East and of the West, it is clear that, by means of the imposition of hands and the words of consecration, the grace of the Holy Spirit is so conferred, and the sacred character so impressed, that bishops in an eminent and visible way undertake Christ's own role as Teacher, Shepherd, and High Priest, and that they act in his person. (Constitution on the Church, #21)

This statement refers to the salvific effect as well as the sacra-mental form of the episcopal consecration.

The effect of the sacrament is twofold: first, the impressing of a sacramental character which makes the recipient like to Christ, and then a fullness of priestly gifts which enable the bishop to carry out his duties in a Christlike spirit. The first has often been understood in a purely static way as a likeness to the Logos-made-flesh, but it is more correct to interpret this character in a dynamic way, as a likening to Christ in regard to his mission, to his active life even up to the obedience unto the cross on Golgotha, and his resurrection. A specific position is created in the Church by the episcopal consecration. It could be said that this ecclesial character is the primary effect and includes the christological character, the likening to the Head of the Church. By the ecclesial and at the same time christological character, the sacrament of consecration creates a differentiation within the People of God. Regarding the second element, it is a question of a particular operation of the Holy Spirit for the fulfilling of that ministry which the character makes both obligatory and possible.

The laying on of hands and prayer are specified as the outward sign of this sacrament. These correspond to the primitive practice of the Church. The putting on of the vestments, which had become common in the early Middle Ages, although it is a demonstration of what is laid upon the bishop, does not properly belong to the sign on which the accomplishment of the sacrament is dependent. Though Jesus himself did not formally specify the sign (since he never formally spoke about the succession), still we can see an indication of it in those texts which show the apostles making provision for successors for the time after their death (1 Tim. 4,14; 2 Tim. 1,6).

The second requirement for membership in the episcopal body, namely the hierarchical "communion" with head and members of the college, forms a whole with the episcopal consecration. It could be said that the consecration is the sacramental ground for the hierarchical communion with head and members, the condition for membership. The two elements, despite their difference, cannot be separated from one another without destroying the whole. If one of the two is missing, a person is no longer a member of the college. This question is further explained by the Council text (Constitution on the Church, #21) which deals with the matter of authority: "Episcopal consecration, together with the office of sanctifying, also confers the offices of teaching and of governing. (These, however, of their very nature, can be exercised only in hierarchical communion with the head and the members of the college.)"

The Council puts the stress on the office of sanctifying, that is, on the ministration of the sacraments. It ascribes to the bishops specifically the power to confer episcopal consecration and thereby to admit newly chosen members into the body of bishops. The offices of teaching and governing are mentioned in second place. They are evidently rooted in the ministry of sanctifying, that is, in the empowering of the bishops to administer the sacraments. They have on their part a sacramental basis, not only because they are mediated by the episcopal consecration but also inasmuch as they have their root in the very sacramental existence of the bishops. The Council speaks of three gifts, indicating that we are not to understand "office" in its strict sense, but rather as an empowerment and commission to a sanctifying ministry. In the sentence cited above, the idea is conspicuous that these offices, namely of teaching and of governing, of their very nature cannot be exercised except in the hierarchical communion with head and members.

It is a question whether this hierarchical communion is required for the accomplishment, and therefore for the validity, of such ministry, or only for its lawfulness; whether, therefore, one who is excluded from the community of bishops can still perform valid though illegitimate acts.

The prefatory note is particulary important for this point. It says:

In consecration is given an ontological participation in sacred functions, as is clear beyond doubt from tradition, even liturgical. The word "functions" is deliberately employed, rather than "powers," since this latter word could be understood as "ready to go into action." But for such ready power to be had, it needs canonical or juridical determination by hierarchical authority. This determination of power can consist in the granting of a particular office, or in an assignment of subjects; and it is given according to norms approved by the highest authority. Such an ulterior norm is demanded by the nature of the case, since there is question of functions which must be exercised by several subjects working together by Christ's will in a hierarchical manner. It is clear that this "communion" has been in the life of the Church according to circumstances of the times, before it was, so to speak, codified in law.

Therefore it is significantly stated that hierarchical communion is required with the head of the Church and its members. Communion is an idea which was held in high honor by the ancient Church (as it is even today, especially in the East). It is understood, however, not of a certain vague feeling, but of an organic reality which demands a juridical form, and is simultaneously animated by charity.

Section 24 of the Constitution on the Church discusses the canonical mission of the bishop. This "can come about through legitimate customs which have not been revoked by the supreme and universal authority of the Church, or by laws made or recognized by that same authority, or directly through the successor of Peter himself. If the latter refuses or denies apostolic communion, a bishop cannot assume office."

In this text two things are seen: first, that the episcopal consecration itself does not suffice for the exercise of the office of teacher and shepherd, but that a corresponding office is required, and that the ministry of teaching and governing has an ontological-sacramental basis. The jurisdictional element is rooted in the sacramental. But in order that the office of shepherd can be

carried out concretely, still another element is required, namely
the hierarchical communion with head and members. This communion includes the so-called canonical mission. This again can
take on different forms, changing its face in the course of history.
It should be noted that the Constitution recognizes custom, so
long as it is not revoked, as a norm of canonical mission. The
usage of the Eastern Church can be seen reflected in this
statement.

In the light of our earlier considerations, it is understandable
that the Council places the power of jurisdiction in the sacramental sphere; this, however, is not a sufficient basis for its
execution in the concrete. For according to traditional teaching,
the sacramental character of likeness to Christ which produces
the sacramental authorization is indelible, while the power of
governing can be lost or removed. Moreover, in the actual
situation of the Church we see that there are many, namely the
titular bishops, who do not have the office of governing, or who
possess it only within a very limited compass. The institution of
the titular bishop has its origin in the loss of an episcopal see on
the part of a bishop as well as in the increasing responsibilities of
the office of bishop or pope, requiring the assistance of another
bishop for their administration. The prefatory note adds that for
the sake of order, "because there are many who have the
episcopal power," the training of individuals in the particular
ministry of governing is necessary.

The fact that despite the close connection between the ministries of sanctifying, teaching, and governing, the power of
jurisdiction must be conferred by a special act, namely the
canonical mission, arises from the other fact that the power of
orders conferred by episcopal consecration is always and in
every case the same, whereas in the sphere of governing there are
hierarchical degrees. Besides the pope, we distinguish patriarchs
and metropolitans. These oversee particular bishoprics. This
peculiarity, which has no counterpart in the secular sphere, is
based upon the fact that the local churches are not only parts of
the whole, but in their own sphere are the whole Church (K.
Mörsdorf).

The emphasis placed on hierarchical communion brings up the

question whether the ministry of sanctifying does not become impossible when a bishop is excluded from the communion with head and members. Concretely, the question is: Can such a bishop still consecrate the bread and wine in the Eucharist or ordain a priest? In traditional theology this question was answered affirmatively without much reflection. It is doubtful, though, whether this view is completely certain. The early Church placed great weight upon communion with head and members. It was, above all, a community—sacramentally in the celebration of the Eucharist, in the same faith in Christ, and in the Holy Spirit. Augustine, in his controversy with the Donatists, represented the view that schismatics could place the outward signs of the sacrament, but that these remained empty, because only one in the true Church could participate in the Holy Spirit.

THE DUTIES OF THE BISHOP

The Proclamation of the Gospel

According to the Constitution on the Church of Vatican II, and as already stated by the Council of Trent, the chief duty of a bishop appointed to a local see or to a community of persons is the *preaching of the gospel.* In this he fulfills his primary responsibility of sanctifying. This has precedence over all other works. The bishops are messengers of faith. They are witnesses to Christ—to his death, resurrection, and second coming. In this formulation there is ascribed to the "Word" a fundamental and comprehensive meaning. The Church here appears as the Church of the Word. This corresponds to the revelation given in Christ, for Jesus Christ is none other than the eternal Word incarnate. We recall the beginning of the Epistle to the Hebrews, that in former times God has spoken in many ways, but now in Christ he has himself spoken his word to men (Heb. 1,1f.). This designation of revelation as revelation in word, or of the Church as the Church of the Word, is not meant to exclude the element of "sign" or lessen its importance. The word itself is in fact an efficacious sign. In Jesus Christ the Word is made visible. In the sacrament, the word and the thing become an integral whole. The sacramental signs, in turn, are visible words. From all this it is seen that preaching has first place among all the duties. In this connection we have the saying of Paul that he was not sent to baptize but to preach (1 Cor. 1,17). The proclamation of the word includes the communication of divine life. It is essentially more than the giving of information. In this connection what was said above about the pope also holds true of the bishop: both have the gravest obligation to preserve the Christian revelation in the light of the Spirit of truth and to expound it faithfully. The bishops, too, must employ suitable means in order to understand revelation in its full depth and breadth, so that they can proclaim it to the faithful. The effort expended on this must, according to the Constitution on the Church (#25), correspond to the gravity of the obligation and the importance of the reality.

The Liturgy

The bishops fulfill their mission of proclamation preeminently in the Eucharist. This is the pronouncement in word and sign, the realization of the central mystery of the Christian faith (Constitution on the Church, #26). Every eucharistic celebration is presided over either by the bishop himself or by someone delegated by him. The Church itself is represented in the eucharistic feast, for it is the memorial celebration of her Lord, of his death and resurrection. Here the Church appears as the Church of Christ, as his Body, as the People of his heavenly Father. In the eucharistic assembly the Church becomes an event, and at the same time this event of the Church happens. In the Eucharist the Church is ever renewed, becomes ever increasingly what she always is, namely the Body of Jesus Christ. The Council says (Constitution on the Church, #26): "In these communities, though frequently small and poor, or living far from any other, Christ is present. By virtue of Him the one, holy, catholic, and apostolic Church gathers together." In the eucharistic celebration, through the memorial, liturgical actions, the bishop proclaims the death and resurrection of Jesus Christ as the salvation-event in which the assembled community takes part. By eating the Lord's body and drinking his blood the whole community is led into a renewed and deepened fraternal unity

Leadership

As leader of the community in the eucharistic meal and sacrifice in which Jesus Christ is present as eschatological Savior, the bishop must be concerned for the order which is proper to a community called to this celebration, as well as for the central event itself of the liturgy. This means he must issue laws, pass judgments, and regulate those things that are necessary for the life of the community. In this capacity he does not act as chairman of a secular administrative area, nor as official or deputy of the pope, but in his own right with the direct power which is his. This authority grows from sacramental ground. It is a "power" which is ordered to service. Only in serving does it have meaning and legitimacy. It is only in order that the ministry of salvation shall be carried out that there is a bishop's office. The bishop should clearly show the example of the Good Shepherd, who came not to be served but to serve (cf. Mt. 20,28; Mk. 10,45) and to give his life for his sheep (cf. Jn. 10,11). He should not refuse to listen to his brethren. His care should extend also to those who do not yet belong, or no longer belong, to the eucharistic community (cf. Rom. 1,14–15).

‹16

Priest and Deacon

DEVELOPMENT OF THE PRIESTHOOD

As we implied in our definition of the bishop in the foregoing chapter, the priestly rank, with its origin in Christ, is actualized in a decisive way in the bishop: the bishop is simply the Priest. Just as the apostles carried out the commission of Jesus Christ through assistants whom they appointed, so also the bishops, successors of the apostles, appointed helpers.

This thesis of the Second Vatican Council (Constitution on the Church, #28) contains obvious problems. The bishops as successors of the apostles have appointed men to assist them, to whom they have given a share in their own authority and commission. In doing this they have prepared the way for a division of authority in the Church. How this came about in history is difficult to determine precisely; probably the question will never be answered with complete certainty. It can be established that even in apostolic times a division of ministries and powers took place. The names which were used for the helpers of the apostles live on in the titles later given to Church functionaries, but this usage does not have exactly the same meaning as it did in apostolic times. This holds true especially of the word "priest." It is derived from the Greek *presbyteros* ("elder"), but it has a somewhat different meaning from the word "presbyter." However, the reality is more important than the terminology. We can recognize the beginning of a hierarchical organization towards

168

the end of the apostolic period first in the Jerusalem church, then
in the Johannine churches and finally also in the Pauline, but it
becomes more distinct in the post-apostolic age, not only in the
churches of Syria but also in Asia Minor. We have evidence for it
in the *Didache* and in the letters of Ignatius of Antioch. Although
Ignatius does not give us any information as to how the duties of
the presbyter are to be understood, we do learn the two following
facts. Apparently the breakdown into different ranks of the
powers proper to the apostles began even in apostolic times. It
was continued in varying degrees by the men appointed by the
apostles as their successors, and from such distinction of degree
developed the later division of powers and duties into different
ranks. The second fact to be remembered is that although we
have no evidence in Scripture that Christ himself ordained a
division of powers of this kind, the possibility of such a division
does lie within the realm of Christian revelation. It devolves,
then, upon the Church to decide to what extent it wants to
develop and perpetuate such a division for the future.

To these basic considerations should be added the historical
fact that this organization was conditioned by the growth of
Christianity. The gospel was preached first of all in the cities; the
first believers were city-dwellers. As the number of believers
became greater, the single bishop of the city was constrained to
commission the members of the *presbyterium* (the bishop's
council) of that city with the priestly care of their individual
districts. But the need for something of this kind became most
evident as the message of Christianity was carried to the country,
and local churches began to spring up outside the cities. The
bishop of the city had to send elders of his own council to the
churches in the country in order to take care of baptisms and the
eucharistic celebrations, as well as the other concerns connected
with the spread of the gospel. Those delegated by him possessed
only a limited power. In the name and at the command of the
bishop they performed the liturgy and did other tasks assigned
them by the bishop. Finally it came about that the elders, instead
of going out from the city from time to time to perform particular
tasks, resided there and, authorized by the bishop, took care of
the ministry entrusted to them. From the third century on, these

local churches took on a greater independence, extending and securing their authority. The relation to the bishop was reduced more and more to the juridical realm, and the sacramental basis of the episcopal power and the sacramental nature of the episcopal consecration were more and more lost sight of.

For the transmitting of a juridical power it seemed that sacramental consecration was not required. From the time of Peter Lombard the teaching was defended and handed down that episcopal consecration was not a sacrament; that the power of the bishop was directed toward the Church as the mystical body, and the power of the priest to the Church as the eucharistic body. The discussion on the matter has, of course, never been ended. Long before Vatican II a large number of theologians inclined to the opinion that episcopal consecration was a sacrament, that it was in fact "the" sacrament of priestly ordination. They thought that this interpretation would have the effect of reestablishing the unity of the power of orders and the power of jurisdiction as it is found in the Fathers.

If, on the slight foundation for it in Scripture, the Church could establish the priesthood as distinct from the office of bishop, then it is clear that should the state of affairs seem to require it, the Church could undertake far-reaching changes to the end that the local church should once more be identical with the bishop's church to a much greater extent than is now the case.

PRIESTLY ORDINATION

Through the sacrament of holy orders a Christian is formed after the image of Christ as the eternal high priest (Heb. 5,1–10; 7,24; 9,11–28). This likeness to Christ received in holy orders is the same as that of the bishop, although it has its own mode proper to the priest. It is an indelible mark, with both an ecclesial and christological aspect. It rests upon the mark of baptism but modifies this in a specific way.

The transmission of priestly powers on the part of the bishop has the character of a sacrament. It is included in the complete sacrament of consecration, for by this act the power of sanctifying is bestowed. The transmission of power occurs through imposition of hands and prayer.

THE DUTIES OF THE PRIEST

In speaking of the ministry of the priest (Constitution on the Church, #28), the Council presents a parallel with that of the bishop. The duties proper to the rank of priest are similar to those of the bishop. The Council enumerates them as follows: preaching of the gospel, pastoral care of the faithful, celebration of the liturgy. This threefold priestly ministry constitutes a participation in the single mediatorship of Jesus Christ (1 Tim. 2,5). It should be brought out here that first place is given to the *preaching of the gospel*. The word has a more comprehensive significance than the sign. Even in the sacramental liturgy it plays the most important role.

The Second Vatican Council also states that the priest exercises his sacred power chiefly at the Eucharist. Here he acts in the person of Christ. He announces the mystery of Christ's salvation, of his saving death and resurrection. He is the leader in the Church's central solemnities, but he can take up this leadership only as assigned by the bishop. Without the participation of the priest there is no genuine Eucharist, not only because his presence is required for the ordered proceeding of the liturgy but also essentially because only he, by pronouncing the words, "This is my body; this is my blood," can make Jesus Christ really present in the Mass. The mode of this presence of Jesus Christ will be discussed in another connection, but it should be noted here that the meaning of the ontological presence of Jesus Christ lies in the fact that the events of Golgotha and of Easter are made present. The ontological presence is the vehicle of the dynamic presence, of his saving presence, of his sacrificial surrender to the Father and of the glorification attained in his resurrection. By the reenactment of the death and resurrection of Jesus Christ in the midst of the People of God, the surrender of Jesus to the Father also becomes present and attainable for those in attendance. They can enter here and now into the sacrificial action of their Head and so go to the Father through Jesus Christ, to the extent that they surrender themselves to the Father. According to Augustine, this self-surrender to the Father is the meaning of the word which the Christian faithful offer in the Eucharist to the

Father. In it they recognize Jesus Christ, the One who died on the cross and was called by the Father in the resurrection to a new life, as their representative before the Father, and thus they attain a share in his own surrender to God. So in the Eucharist they realize their existence as Christian men. This concept of the Eucharist reveals what the Council means when it says that in the local assembly of the faithful celebrating the Eucharist, the universal Church is made visible. And this is true not only of the bishop's church but of every local church. In the local church, the Church as the body of Christ, as messianic and eschatological community, continually becomes an event again, and it cannot do so in any other way with the same intensity and concreteness. It must be said of the priest who is not a bishop that because of his function in the eucharistic celebration, he also is responsible for the order of the eucharistic community outside the celebration. His responsibility consists in seeking ever to form the Church into a fraternal community, and he does this not only by his word but also by example. Under this guise the Council calls him not only father but also brother of the members of the community.

Since the priest is commissioned by the bishop to celebrate the central mystery of the Church and thus the Church becomes an event in a particular place, the priest should always remain conscious of this association with the bishop, just as the bishop, for his part, should always regard his priestly co-workers as brothers and friends. And because of their common duties and responsibilities the priests should always form a real community among themselves. In union with their bishop they constitute a single *presbyterium*.

The powers of the priest are understood correctly only when they are seen as powers for service. But this means that priests, as well as bishops, should not act in the manner of secular authorities. The basic principle of the order for which they are responsible is love, whose original form is the self-abandonment of Jesus Christ on the cross for his brothers and sisters. Under this aspect, it must be emphasized once again, freedom has the priority. No limits can be imposed on it except those which are required by good order, that is, by the love of the brothers for one another.

THE DEACON

Referring to deacons, as mentioned in Scripture, the Council states (Constitution on the Church, #29) that the diaconate is not to be considered merely a preparatory rank for the priesthood but should again assume the independent function which it had in the early Church. The duties of the deacon are manifold. He can be assigned all those tasks which do not require ordination, which means everything except the consecration of the Mass and the administration of penance, confirmation, and extreme unction.

In actual fact, however, the tasks assigned to the deacon are ones which can be carried out by every Christian, and so assigning them to the deacon would seem to require a special unnecessary sacramental ordination. So it must be examined further, how far the diaconate can be reactivated without excluding the laity from their proper active role in the Church.

‹ 17

The Bishop of Rome as Peter's Successor

THE IDEA OF SUCCESSION

Succession to Peter has a different structure from succession to the other apostles. As an individual, Peter can have only one single successor. The incumbent bishop of Rome is, according to the declared belief of the Catholic Church, the successor of the apostle Peter. But with relation to the other apostles, the incumbent of one particular bishopric is not the successor of one particular apostle. There are not just eleven bishops, as there were twelve—or eleven—apostles. In the early Church, it is true, a special authority belonged to those bishoprics which could trace their origin directly to one of the apostles. However, those bishops who had been appointed by one of the apostles' successors and set over a church which was not directly apostolic were also considered as legitimate witnesses of the tradition. Irenaeus and Tertullian used the idea of succession for such bishops also. Although the bishop who occupies a see originally founded by an apostle can be considered in a certain sense a successor to the apostle, nevertheless all the bishops, as a body, succeed the body of apostles, even though in no case can it be said from which particular apostle an episcopal consecration is derived. The entire college of bishops represents the succession to the entire college of the apostles. Each single bishop, as a consequence of his admission to the episcopal college, stands in an historical, if no longer directly traceable, line of succession to the apostles. This is the crucial point, that in the faith of the Church, the episcopal college of today, consisting of many individual bishops, constitutes the body of successors to the twelve men who composed the college of the apostles.

THE PRIMACY

Here there are three questions to be discussed: (1) Has Peter had a successor at all? (2) Who is that successor? (3) What is the meaning of such succession? (The further question—so important for the context of our problem—of the relation of the pope to the other bishops has already been discussed in connection with the episcopacy.)

THE FACT OF SUCCESSION

As we have seen earlier, nothing is reported in Scripture to the effect that Jesus had appointed a successor to Peter, or that he told Peter himself to appoint one. But what was said of the apostolic succession holds also here in the case of Peter, namely, that the succession is a "given" by the nature of the situation. The thesis of the apostolic succession is established by an analysis of the fullness of powers given to Peter. Although his situation is unique, his mission was to be carried on till the end of time. We must reflect on the words of Jesus, analyzing the commission given to Peter. Jesus promised Peter that he would be the rock on which the Church was founded. He is not speaking here of a passing thing, but of the enduring quality of the foundation. It belongs to the essence of the Church that the foundation on which it is built should remain forever. The indestructibility of the Church is guaranteed, according to the words of Christ, by this very fact of the indestructibility of its foundation. When we pass from the figure to the reality, it follows that Peter can be the foundation of the Church only if he leads and directs Christ's messianic community in such a way that it effectively endures. It is consistent with this concept of the Church as a rock that the members are called living stones, out of which the house of the Church is built (1 Pet. 2,5), and that Paul speaks of the temple of the Holy Spirit (1 Cor. 3,16; Eph. 2,22). If the figure gives a static impression, the dynamic must be introduced when the metaphor is translated into the real. If imperishability is guaranteed through sure direction and leadership, this must be accomplished until the coming of the Lord. There must, then, be those who carry that responsibility and power of Peter's until the coming of the Lord, if the existence of the Church is to be as secure as that of a house built upon rock. The same considerations hold for the image of the keys, as well as that of binding and loosing.

WHY THE BISHOP OF ROME?

We come then to the second question: Who is the successor of Peter? In the faith-understanding of the Catholic Church, the bishop of Rome is the successor of Peter. So immediately there follows the question, Why the bishop of Rome? The most obvious answer is that Peter himself was in Rome and there suffered a martyr's death. But there is a question contained in this answer—whether Peter really was in Rome and why he was there. The fact of Peter's Roman sojourn is today accepted by not a few Protestant theologians; yet, at the same time, in other quarters it is disputed as vehemently as ever. With regard to the arguments for such a sojourn, the first point to be noted is that according to Acts, Peter, after his miraculous release from prison, went off to "another place" (Acts 12,17). The place itself is not named. As we have seen once before, Peter appeared in Antioch and remained there for a time. We know from both Acts and the Epistle to the Galatians (Gal. 2,11.14) that he worked among the Jews. This limiting of his mission to the Jews cannot, however, be taken too strictly. The more his activity was extended beyond Palestine into Syria, and perhaps Asia Minor and still farther, the more impossible would it be for him to attend merely to the Jews and not also to the Gentiles. As a matter of fact, it was Peter who was the first to receive a Gentile into the Christian community (Acts 10).

That Peter did go to Rome and there died a martyr's death under Nero is confirmed by the following observations. The conclusion of the First Epistle of Peter (5,13) runs: "Greetings from her who dwells in Babylon, chosen by God like you." Babylon can only mean Rome; it must be taken as a symbolic pseudonym for this city (cf. Rev. 14,8; 16,9; 17,5.18; 18,2.10.21; 19,2).

Further evidence for the sojourn of Peter in Rome is given us by Ignatius of Antioch, Dionysius of Corinth, the Roman priest Gaius, and Irenaeus. When Ignatius of Antioch was on his way to martyrdom at Rome, he sent a letter ahead to his brothers in the faith in which he says (*Ignatius to the Romans*, 4,3): "Not as Peter and Paul do I send you instructions. For they were apostles; I am a condemned man. They were free; I am now a slave."

According to Dionysius of Corinth, a portion of whose writings have been preserved for us by Eusebius, both apostles, Peter and Paul, had taught in Italy and there together suffered martyrdom. The Roman presbyter Gaius is reported by Eusebius to have said: "I can show you the trophies of the apostles. For if you would like to go to the Vatican hill or walk along the road to Ostia, you will see the trophies of those who founded this Church." By "trophies" is to be understood the markers over the graves.

According to Irenaeus—who came from Asia Minor, then went to Rome and became Bishop of Lyons, and is therefore a witness to a tradition spread throughout the whole Church—both apostles, Peter and Paul, established the Church at Rome. The excavations at San Sebastian on the Appian Way and also under St. Peter's seem to attest to the presence of Peter in Rome. So there are no absolutely conclusive proofs for the stay of Peter in Rome, but there is weighty evidence which has not been overturned by any historical objection.

Why Peter went to Rome is a different question. No reason is given in Scripture. Was it an actual command of Jesus, or a special illumination of the Holy Spirit—a revelation—or a purely human insight into the importance of the Roman capital for the spread of Christianity? The last two elements could be considered as one, inasmuch as the activity of the Holy Spirit in apostolic times accounts for the process of revelation, and the Spirit of God can make use of the natural situation. Therefore, if Peter went to Rome in these circumstances—that is, as the chief of the apostles directed by the Holy Spirit—one could speak of a divine revelation. The answer to our question is very important, because it makes the association of the primacy with Rome of divine origin if it goes back to the Spirit which was sent by Christ and which constituted Peter as the head of the apostles. In any case, Rome would be a particularly favorable center for the spread of Christianity because of its importance as the capital of the Roman empire and its consequent attraction for the many religious movements of that time.

Probably in the year 58 Paul departed from Jerusalem to go to Rome (Acts 23,11); earlier, in Corinth, he had often expressed his intention to travel to Rome (Rom. 1,13).

Knowing himself to be the one commissioned by Jesus Christ to open the door of the Church to the Gentiles, it was natural that Peter should choose the headquarters of the ancient world as his seat, especially since other cities offered no such incentive. Jerusalem was nearing its end; Antioch (in the backwoods of Syria), Ephesus (in the backwoods of Asia Minor), the Greek cities with their ancient history, had for a long time been standing in the shadow of Rome. Their cultures also were being used in the service of Rome. If the Spirit, the salvific power of Jesus Christ operative in the Church, can really be called the soul of the Church, then surely an impulse of the Spirit could not have been lacking in this decision of Peter's. On the other hand, the decision was not taken out of his hands.

One can ask whether the fact of Peter's stay in Rome is so essential that without it there would be no foundation for the primacy of the bishop of Rome. The answer is disputed. It is possible to think of the establishment of the Church's center at Rome, carrying on the work of Peter, as based on a decision of the Church itself.

The question whether the primacy can ever be dissociated from the bishopric of Rome is in the same category. This question is likewise disputed in Catholic theology. It goes without saying that the bishop of Rome can move his seat of government to another city: what is in question is whether a "legal" change would be possible whereby the bishop of another see could become the successor of the apostle Peter. If the establishment of the primacy in Rome was done by the Church, there does not seem to be any reason why the Church could not change it.

‹ 18

Papal Primacy: the Development of the Doctrine; the Concepts and Practices of the Popes

THE DEVELOPMENT OF THE PRIMACY—
EVOLUTION OF THE DOCTRINE

Although the idea that the bishop of Rome is the successor of Peter is part of the Church's faith, this does not mean that today's concept of the primacy is necessarily the same as that which prevailed at the beginning of the process of development. The designation "pope" in its Latin or Greek form was originally used for the superiors of monasteries and for bishops, later especially for patriarchs. From the middle of the fourth century it has been applied to the bishop of Rome (it was first used of Siricius). In the Western Church the title has been reserved to the bishop of Rome since the end of Christian antiquity. Is it conceivable that a Christian from the first or second century would recognize in today's papacy the precedence of the apostle Peter with which he was familiar in his own age?

With the passage of time the form of the primacy has changed as much as has the external appearance of the whole Church. The change has been conditioned by circumstances, by the overlaying of social, cultural, and political elements upon the original structure; but it has also derived from the personal impress of the

180

men who have held the office. The external aspect of the office and its mode of execution are subject to far-reaching historical modification. In the Eastern Church, for example, whose structure was subject to historical influences differing from those which prevailed in the West, many sovereign functions which in the Latin Church belong to the Pope are assigned to the patriarchs.

Passing beyond the evidence for the primacy and its historical development for the moment, we observe that early in history various ranks of bishoprics arose, owing to the preeminence of one see over another because the former had been founded by an apostle or had greater missionary strength. Thus large associations of churches with one hierarchical head came into being. Since the fifth and sixth centuries these have been called patriarchates. In the Eastern Church, in association with the civil organization, ecclesiastical provinces were formed which were headed by metropolitans. According to a ruling of the Council of Nicea (A.D. 325), the rights and privileges of the patriarchs were not to be encroached upon by this development. The bishops of Rome, Alexandria, and Antioch were expressly mentioned. The supreme authority of these chief bishops was exercised in the ordination and the recalling of bishops and in presiding at the synods in which decisions concerning disputed matters were made.

Although the manifestations of the primacy of the see of Rome during the first century are often faint and unclear, we can find some evidence for it. The first such evidence is the letter to which we have already referred, sent to the church in Corinth by the church of Rome (and written by one of its presbyters, Clement) toward the end of the century (A.D. 96?). The occasion for the epistle was the rebellion of some (as the letter calls them) bold men against the elders of the Corinthian church, and its object was to restore peace and to reestablish in the Corinthian community the fervor for which it had formerly been renowned in all the churches. The Roman church does this unasked and uninvited, wholly on its own initiative. The letter, as its title indicates, is written in the name of the whole Roman community: "The church of God which lives as a stranger at Rome," Clement writes, "to the church of God which lives as a stranger at Corinth, the ones called, sanctified by the will of God through our Lord Jesus Christ." It is true that this epistle does not represent a formal, authoritative intervention by which the Corinthians would be legally bound and obliged. The author calls his directions a counsel, and he includes himself in the obligation to repentance and amendment to which he invites the Corinthians. However, the tone is more than merely admonitory when he calls for subordination among the presbyters and does it in language which is expressive of a consciousness of responsibility and authority. He demands obedience to what he has written in the Holy Spirit: no other community had felt itself responsible in this way for a brother community. This letter of Clement's gives evidence of a particular attitude of authority, of the claim of the community of Rome to a distinctive position among the other Christian communities. It is to be noted that subsequently an extraordinary importance was ascribed to it throughout the universal Church: indeed it was widely regarded as part of the New Testament.

Soon afterwards Ignatius of Antioch singled out the Christian community of Rome for the highest praise. The most important title which he gives the Roman community is "presider in love." Here the expression "love" may be understood not as a designation of the whole Church, but as a radically new thing which came into the world with Christ and constitutes the innermost essence of Christianity. Although the phrase "the presider in love" does not signify any legal precedence of the Roman community, it does, nevertheless, indicate a superiority over the other communities. As Ignatius says, with reference to the epistle of Clement, the Roman community instructs others, but does not itself receive instruction. Ignatius gives directions and advice to other communities, but he does not presume to give admonition to the Roman community. Instead, he begs it to receive the church in Syria as Christ, and after the manner of the bishop. According to Ignatius, the underlying reason for the reputation and precedence of the Roman community is the fact that Peter and Paul had lived in it and had there preached the gospel.

Irenaeus of Lyons was concerned with defending the mainstream of Christian tradition against the Gnostics. It is very instructive that he refutes Gnosticism not by an exposition of its inner contradictions and falseness, but rather by showing that its representatives did not have the apostolic succession. For he sees in the apostolic succession the guarantee of the true Christian teaching; looking backward, it is clear that the teaching of Christ is transmitted by the bishops in a succession which reverts ultimately to the apostles. It would, however, be too involved to enumerate all the churches founded by the apostles and to investigate their traditions. It is sufficient if it is proved of the largest, oldest, best-known churches and of those founded by the glorious apostles Peter and Paul, including Rome, that the line of their bishops goes back to the apostles, and therefore that their teaching is apostolic. "With this church, because of its more powerful preeminence *(propter potentiorem principalitatem)*, all other churches in all other places must be in agreement, since in it Christians of all places have the apostolic tradition preserved" (*Against the False Gnosis*, III,3,3). Taken in conjunction with the context in itself and a parallel passage in the fourth book (3,2), the Latin words supplied here have the unequivocal sense of a "higher apostolicity." The apostolicity of the Roman church is preeminent in relation to that of the other churches because it goes back to the apostles. Here, on the grounds of its twofold apostolicity, a superiority over all the others is attributed to the Roman church.

Tertullian and Hippolytus go a step further in that they designate Peter alone as the beginning and the source of the line of bishops.

Cyprian sees the unity of the Church founded in Peter. By giving the power of binding and loosing to one man only—namely, Peter—Jesus publicly announced that by his will the Church is one and small remain one. Peter is not only the symbol but also the real ground of this unity. Although Cyprian denies to the bishop of Rome an active primacy of jurisdiction over the other apostles, he sees the power conferred on the other apostles as a participation in the power already conferred on the one man, Peter. Every church is the seat of Peter, but the Roman church is that in a special way.

Optatus of Milevis (d. before 400) went a step further and taught that it was union with the church of Rome which ensured the legitimacy of the other churches.

Although in the texts cited thus far we can see only an embryonic evidence for the Roman primacy, there are clearer expressions of it to be found elsewhere in ancient Christendom, chiefly from the fourth century on. Ambrose, for instance, states: "Where Peter is, there is the Church" (*Comm. on Ps.*, 40,30). Jerome writes to Pope Damasus: "I follow no one as leader except Christ alone, and therefore I want to remain in union in the Church with you, that is, with the chair of Peter. I know that on this rock the Church is founded." (*Letters*, 15,2)

Whereas Augustine did not arrive at a recognition of the Roman primacy during his controversy with the Donatists, this recognition came later on, during his struggle against Pelagianism. After three African synods had condemned Pelagianism he sought with increasing eagerness to obtain the concurrence of Rome; for, he said, only if the apostolic see with its supreme authority gave the stamp of official approval to the decision of the African bishops would they be safeguarded against the dangers which threatened, and only then would those who had been led astray be brought back again to the right path. (*Letters*, 177,19)

It is of great significance that from the second century on, Christians were already turning to Rome when disputes arose, either to secure approval for their own viewpoint or else to establish contact with Rome (e.g., Polycarp of Smyrna in the matter of the date of the Easter celebration, Polycrates of Ephesus, Irenaeus, Hegesippus of Palestine). We are informed about these trips to Rome by the *Ecclesiastical History* of Eusebius. From the fourth century on we encounter these facts: that the bishops sought the protection of Rome in the face of any threat to their rights; that they appealed to Rome in legal matters; and that against the decision of Rome further appeal was inadmissible. The heretics, too, took Rome into account. It is significant, also, that the Roman baptismal rite became the standard, definitive one. Rome had a part in forming the canon of Scripture, and it played a decisive role in the struggles against the Gnostics, the Marcionites, and the Montanists.

The scholastic theologians of the Middle Ages in general treated the problem of the Roman primacy only in the context of other problems—e.g., in connection with the description of priestly ordination or the discussion of the concept of faith, or in the context of the emerging religious orders of the thirteenth century. In late Scholasticism, owing to the difficulties and entanglements involving the papacy, the conciliar theory arose, which assigned to the council, rather the pope, the highest authority in the Church. The unresolved opposition between conciliarism and the doctrine of the papal primacy lasted through the centuries until the First Vatican Council.

The following particulars should be noted. The question of the primacy was raised in the time when Scholasticism was at its height, primarily in regard to the emergence of the new Franciscan and Dominican orders. The new orders were causing a disruption of the established financial and hierarchical systems, inasmuch as the members of the order were subject only to a general superior—not, like the secular clergy, to a bishop or pastor. Since, in financial matters above all, they wanted to be responsible to the pope, the members of religious orders were in a special way "the pope's sons." On the other hand, there was strong objection to this practice in some quarters, especially from Wilhelm of Saint Amour.

Thomas Aquinas conceived the Roman primacy on a monarchic model, as the most perfect form of government. The Church represents a plurality, and therefore, in the interests of unity and peace, it is best governed by one man. Aquinas was evidently influenced in these considerations by the Platonic concept of the One: the pope guarantees the unity of the Church by his teaching authority.

The unity of the Church is also the basic theme of Bonaventure, but he carries it out more inclusively and comprehensively than Thomas Aquinas. For his teaching on the primacy he makes use of the Arabian Aristotelianism of Averroes on the level of form, and on the material level, of the neo-Platonic idea of Pseudo-Dionysius, *reductio.* On both levels, formal and material, according to Bonaventure, there is a first and highest to which all the individuals refer back, and which is the origin and source of all the individuals. The pope is at the apex of the structure built on the ministerial hierarchy. The structure follows the organizing principle: the farther it moves down, the more it is spread out, and the more it moves up, the more it is reduced to unity; so there are many bishops, fewer archbishops, very few patriarchs, and only one pope. He is the only, the first, the highest spiritual father of all the fathers, in fact of all the faithful; he is the head of the hierarchy, the single bridegroom, the highest bishop, the vicar of Christ, the fount, source, and standard of all ecclesiastical sovereignty. From him all authority in the Church is derived, from that of the lowest members in the Church to those claiming higher power and rank in the hierarchy (*Breviloquium*, 6,12). In this teaching on the primacy Bonaventure goes far beyond the statements of the First Vatican Council and of the Second as well. His theory is based more on philosophical-sociological considerations than on theological, although the latter are not lacking.

One theologian from Bonaventure's school, Peter John Olivi, who at first taught a doctrine similar to that of his master, finally, in the course of his defense of the "Spirituals" against the Roman Curia, came to the opinion that the pope is the anti-Christ. In such views we can see the foreshadowing of the attack on the papacy by the Reformers. In post-Tridentine theology, the dogma of the primacy developed more and more into the form which received its final summation at the First Vatican Council.

THE POPE'S UNDERSTANDING OF THE PRIMACY

Within the Church's tradition about the position of the bishop of Rome, the understanding of the one who fills the office and his mode of exercising it are important factors.

Only a few illustrations can be given here. Some of the papal pronouncements were taken up in the full statement of the First Vatican Council. Included here was the statement of the papal envoy before the Council of Ephesus (431), which was accepted unanimously by those present. Another instance is the formula of Pope Hormisdas, the ratification of which by some 250 Eastern bishops ended the Acacian Schism (484–519); it was also accepted later by the eighth ecumenical council (the Fourth Council of Constantinople, 869). Another example is the confession of faith to which the Emperor Michael Palaeologus had his legate swear before the ecumenical council of Lyons (1274). Pope Siricius (384–398? 399) also makes a statement in which he points out that it is the task of his office to bear the burdens of all who are oppressed, since in the Roman bishop Peter himself guards his inheritance. During the Pelagian controversy Innocent I (401–417), writing to the African bishops in a letter of January 27, 417, evoked by Augustine, declares: "In the examination of the affairs of God you have the example of ancient tradition as well as the power of your faith joined securely to reason; inasmuch as you were of the opinion that your affairs should be brought before our judgment, you have true recognition of what is proper to the apostolic see. For from it comes every aspect of the bishop's office and all the authority which is attached to this name."

Perhaps the high-water mark of papal claims to authority was reached with Boniface VIII, who declared in the year 1302, in the Bull *Unam Sanctam:* "Therefore this one and only Church does not have two heads, like some monstrous birth, but rather only one body and one head, Christ and his representative, Peter, and Peter's successor. It is necessary for salvation for all men unconditionally, to be subject to the Roman Pontiff; this we declare, define, and proclaim." (Cf. DS 873–875.)

A number of theses arising out of Wyclif's spiritual conception of the Church and out of the views of his disciple John Hus, all of them denying or denigrating the papacy, were condemned (DS 1207, 1210, 1211, 1212, 1213, 1220, 1222, 1223, 1224, 1226, 1229; cf. 1300–1302). For an understanding of the primacy, the Council of Florence is also of importance (1438–1445, DS 1307) and likewise the eighteenth ecumenical council, the Fifth Lateran (1512–1517: DS 1445) and the Bull *Exsurge, Domine* of July 5, 1520 (DS 1475–1480). (See also the condemnation of Gallicanism and Febronianism, two movements in which the system of conciliarism lived on: DS 2329f., 2281–2285, 2540, 2592–2597, etc.)

THE EXERCISE OF THE PAPACY

The doctrine of the primacy is to be distinguished from the exercise of the primacy. In the second century Pope Victor (189–198) excommunicated the churches in Asia Minor because they refused to accept the Roman date for Easter, and so were causing disunity. He formulated the excommunication in such a way that it was not just a question of himself breaking off association with them, but of his explicitly excluding them from communion with the whole Church. He referred in this connection to the tombs of Peter and Paul in Rome. Pope Stephen I (254–257), who was the first (as far as we can see) to cite Matthew 16,18ff. in this matter, in his conflict with heretics demanded the acceptance of his teaching and threatened with excommunication those who resisted; this, again, with an appeal to the full authority of the apostle Peter, which had been transmitted to his successor.

From the fourth century on, the Roman bishops—especially Siricius (384–398), Innocent I (402–417), and Zosimus (412? – 417–418)—became more definite in their claims about the primacy. Leo the Great (440–461) was most clear and definitive. They express the conviction that as successors to Peter they have a task to fulfill which has been given to them by the Lord of the Church. The extent to which these Roman claims corresponded to the understanding of the whole Church in at least one instance is evident from the Council of Chalcedon (451). Here, as the letter of Pope Leo I was read, the Council's participants exclaimed: "This is the faith of the fathers, this is the faith of the apostles! Through Leo, Peter has spoken." In the documents which the Council addressed to the Pope he is called the interpreter of the voice of the apostle Peter. On this basis Gelasius (492–496) developed the theory of the Two Powers, which led to the Middle Ages to a grave struggle for ultimate dominion between the spiritual and the secular powers.

‹ 19

The First Vatican Council

The debate which has gone on for many centuries now between the conciliar system and the papal system reached a climax at the First Vatican Council, which supported the supreme authority of the pope in matters of faith and morals (against Gallican tendencies) and at the same time laid down limits to the papal power (against exaggerations regarding the temporal power of the popes, arising out of the historic struggles between Church and State).

The structure of patriarchates which characterized the patristic Church and which has been preserved in the East was not abolished by this act. In general, the papacy is meant to function as the supreme judicial authority in matters of faith. In the process of development which went on from the beginning of the Great Eastern Schism (1054), the patriarchal power in the western Church was absorbed into that of the papacy. Bishops were named directly by Rome and stood, without intermediary, under the metropolitan of Rome.

However, if we compare the attitude towards the see and the bishop of Rome in ancient Christianity with that of the First Vatican Council we cannot fail to see that a far-reaching development has taken place.

ITS HISTORICAL SIGNIFICANCE

In view of the magnitude of the problem it seems desirable to cite the most important passages from the First Vatican Council

189

verbatim. This Council sought to provide a profession of faith which would express clearly and completely the Church's understanding of itself. But owing to political circumstances, to the Franco-Prussian War and the Seizure of the Papal States, and also to the fact that this ecclesiology was not yet fully matured, only a portion of the whole was treated—namely, the question of the Roman primacy. Concerning the bishops, the Council contented itself with a redeeming clause which it envisaged as guaranteeing that the authority of the bishops would not be prejudiced by the definition of the primacy.

As the following years made evident, the great stress on the Roman primacy at the First Vatican Council was productive not only of support for the authority of the pope but also of the subsequent excessive development of Roman centralization which today, in a swing of the pendulum, is occasioning the search for a mode of operation of the papacy which will afford the bishops, not just in theory but in practice as well, the exercise of that freedom which belongs to them.

The text of the First Vatican Council states a doctrine and concludes with a definition. While it first makes a statement about the precedence of the apostle Peter, it continues as follows in the second chapter of the dogmatic constitution *Pastor Aeternus* of July 18, 1870:

Now, what Christ the Lord, supreme shepherd and watchful guardian of the flock, established in the person of the blessed apostle Peter for the perpetual safety and everlasting good of the Church must, by the will of the same, endure without interruption in the Church which was founded on the rock and which will remain firm until the end of the world. Indeed, "no one doubts, in fact it is obvious to all ages, that the holy and most Blessed Peter, Prince and head of the Catholic Church, received the keys of the kingdom from our Lord Jesus Christ, the savior and the redeemer of the human race; and even to this time and forever he lives," and governs "and exercises judgment in his successors," the bishops of the holy Roman See, which he established and consecrated with his blood (Council of Ephesus). Therefore, whoever succeeds Peter in this Chair holds Peter's primacy over the whole Church according to the plan of Christ himself. "Therefore, the dispositions made by Truth endure; and St. Peter still has the rocklike strength that has been given to him, and he has not surrendered the helm of the Church with which he was entrusted (Leo the Great). For this reason, "because of its greater sovereignty," it was always "necessary for every church, that is, the faithful who are everywhere, to be in agreement" with the Roman Church (Irenaeus). The outcome of this will be that in this See, from which "the bonds of sacred communion" are imparted to all, the members will be joined as members under one head and thus coalesce into one compact body.

Therefore, if anyone says that it is not according to the institution of Christ our Lord himself, that is, by divine law, that St. Peter has perpetual successors in the primacy over the whole Church; or if anyone says that the Roman Pontiff is not the successor of St. Peter in the same primacy: let him be anathema.

The third chapter continues:

Therefore, relying on the clear testimony of the Holy Scriptures and following the express and definite decrees of Our predecessors, the Roman Pontiffs, and of the general councils, We reaffirm the definition of the ecumenical Council of Florence. According to this definition all the faithful of Christ must believe "that the holy Apostolic See and the Roman Pontiff is the successor of St. Peter, the Prince of the Apostles, and the true vicar of of Christ, the head of the whole Church, the father and teacher of all Christians; and that to him, in the person of St. Peter, was given by our Lord Jesus Christ the full power of feeding, ruling, and governing the whole Church; as is also contained in the proceedings of the ecumenical councils and in the sacred canons."

And so we teach and declare that, in the disposition of God, the Roman Church holds the preeminence of ordinary power over all the other churches; and that this power of jurisdiction of the Roman Pontiff, which is truly episcopal, is immediate. Regarding this jurisdiction, the shepherds of whatever rite and dignity and the faithful, individually and collectively, are bound by a duty of hierarchical subjection and of sincere obedience; and this not only in matters that pertain to faith and morals, but also in matters that pertain to the discipline and government of the Church throughout the whole world. When, therefore, this bond of unity with the Roman Pontiff is guarded both in government and in the profession of the same faith, then the Church of Christ is one flock under one supreme shepherd. This is the doctrine of Catholic truth; and no one can deviate from this without losing his faith and his salvation.

The power of the Supreme Pontiff is far from standing in the way of the power of ordinary and immediate episcopal jurisdiction by which the bishops, who under appointment of the Holy Spirit, succeeded in the place of the apostles, feed and rule individually, as true shepherds, the particular flock assigned to them. Rather this latter power is asserted, confirmed and vindicated by this same supreme and universal shepherd in the words of St. Gregory the Great: "My honor is the honor of the whole Church. My honor is the solid strength of my brothers. I am truly honored when due honor is paid to each and every one." . . .

And because, by the divine right of apostolic primacy, the Roman Pontiff is at the head of the whole Church, We also teach and declare that he is the supreme judge of the faithful and that one can have recourse to his judgment in all cases pertaining to ecclesiastical jurisdiction. We declare that the judgment of the Apostolic See, whose authority is unsurpassed, is not subject to review by anyone; nor is anyone allowed to pass judgment on its decision. Therefore, those who say that it is permitted to appeal to an ecumenical council from the decisions of the Roman Pontiff (as to an authority superior to the Roman Pontiff) are far from the straight path of truth.

And so, if anyone says that the Roman Pontiff has only the office of inspection or direction, but not the full and supreme power of jurisdiction over the whole Church, not only in matters that pertain to faith and morals, but also in matters that pertain to the discipline and government of the Church throughout the whole world; or if anyone says that he has only a more important part and not the complete fullness of this supreme power; or if anyone says that this power is not ordinary and immediate either over each and every church or over each and every shepherd and faithful member: let him be anathema.[1] (DS 3053–3064)

Other statements about the papal primacy are to be found in the encyclical letter of Pius XII on the Mystical Body of Christ, as well as in many documents of the Second Vatican Council. None of these, however, goes beyond the exposition of the First Vatican Council.

We turn now to the interpretation of the Council's pronouncements. There is a certain indefiniteness in some of the texts, inasmuch as they do not speak of the pope but of the apostolic see, and it is unclear whether the latter expression means the

[1]The translation of these passages and those which follow from the First Vatican Council is taken from *The Church Teaches* (St. Louis, Herder, 1955).

pope himself. Since it is generally accepted that the papal power
as such cannot be delegated, this is not a trivial question.

EXPOSITION

For a right understanding of the teaching of the First Vatican
Council it is of fundamental importance that the christological
basis of the pope's primacy be seen. According to the teaching of
Vatican I, the papacy was founded in Christ's commissioning of
the apostle Peter. The Council leaves open the question of the
connection between the commission to Peter and the primacy of
the Roman Pontiff, giving no formal explanation as to how the
succession to Peter came about in the history of the Church.
Instead, it contents itself simply with the faith-statement that the
bishop of Rome as successor to Peter possesses universal, true
episcopal power, the full and highest authority in the Church. He
is not merely the first among equals, but rather he has the right,
consonant with his office, to issue directives which must be
obeyed in faith. His jurisdiction extends to all the members of the
Church. He can give orders which bind the whole Church and
every individual in it. He is dependent neither upon the whole
college of bishops nor upon the bishop of any one place. The
deepest reason for the binding nature of the papal primacy is its
origin in Jesus Christ, that is to say, its "divine" character. The
pope acts as the vicar of Christ. In a certain sense, of course, this
holds true also for the other bishops, in accordance with the
principle of the "Shaliach": "The one sent is as good as the one
sending." They are, however, competent only for their own part
of the Church. The direction of the whole Church belongs to the
pope because of his empowerment by Christ.

RELATIONSHIP TO CHRIST

A very important statement is made, namely, that the pope is the
representative of Jesus Christ, the invisible head of the Church. If
and to the extent that Christ is active here and now in the dealings
of the pope, Christ himself is making demands on men through

the papal actions. In him the members of the Church hear the voice of the Lord in the concrete circumstances of life and history. But this thesis cannot be rightly understood without taking into account the thrust of the human element. The Church has not two heads but one, insofar as the invisible head, Jesus Christ, is represented by the pope as visible head. All power in the Church stems from Christ. Without Christ or apart from him there is no power. All the fullness of this power deriving from Christ and given by him to the Church is united in the pope. Jesus Christ, represented and made visible in the pope, is to be understood as the glorified Lord, ever present and active in the Holy Spirit in the Church. The emphasis on this relation to Christ does not, of course, exclude the spontaneity, freedom, and personal style of each individual pope.

With regard to those few pronouncements of the pope for which infallibility is claimed, Christ himself vouches for the truth, and yet the expression of it will certainly be marked by the human manner of the pope. In purely jurisdictional acts and the ordinary teaching which is not infallible, Christ's use of the human being becomes still clearer, and here we may and must distinguish even more carefully between Christ and the human vessel. Such papal pronouncements, as expressions of the pope, have great weight, but they are changeable, and the possibility of such modification must be taken into account.

PERSONAL INDIVIDUALITY

There is an extraordinary scope for the exercise of personal individuality by the pope, despite his calling to be the instrument of Christ and to represent him. A look at Church history gives ample corroboration of this fact. It can happen, for instance, that a pope gives to a faith-statement which is founded in Holy Scripture and of special concern to him an accent which is not in Scripture, and thus, without any actual denial of Christian truth, the whole order of faith and its detailed parts fall into a particular perspective. An outstanding example of this was the Second Vatican Council, which made no new statements (new with respect to content) concerning the self-understanding of the

Church, but put the Church in a different perspective and so shed a new light on many individual doctrines.

THE SACRAMENTALITY OF THE CHURCH

Since it is Christ who acts in the activity of the pope and so appears to the eye of faith within human history, it can be seen that the authority of the pope is rooted in the sacramentality of the entire Church. The sacramentality consists in this, that through Christ present in the Holy Spirit as the life principle of the Church, God communicates himself salvifically in the shape of tangible, visible signs, by means of men, events, and things. (The bishop's power of jurisdiction is also rooted in the sacramentality of the Church.) If there is any act of the Church which does not partake of its sacramentality, it will be sin or error. But even such an act would not be neutral in this respect, but rather would represent a resistance to the sacramental character of the Church. The primacy partakes in the sacramentality of the messianic People of God. These connections are brought out in their full scope in the Scriptures, as the passages quoted below will show. First of all we can say: What the glorified Jesus communicated to all the apostles after his resurrection holds also for the apostle Peter, although the power bestowed on him exceeded that of the others. John declares (Jn. 20,19–22): "Late that Sunday evening, when the disciples were together behind locked doors, for fear of the Jews, Jesus came and stood among them, 'Peace be with you!' he said, and then showed them his hands and his side. So when the disciples saw the Lord, they were filled with joy. Jesus repeated, 'Peace be with you!' and then said, 'As the Father sent me, so I send you.' " The gospel continues: "He then breathed on them, saying, 'Receive the Holy Spirit! If you forgive any man's sins, they stand forgiven; if you pronounce them unforgiven, unforgiven they remain.' " The peace meant here is peace with God and peace with one another. It is the greatest good among the gifts of salvation. Only those united with Christ in the Holy Spirit are called to dispense to others that salvation which is the gift of Jesus Christ.

The same direction is indicated when Jesus, in giving Simon

Peter his special commission, puts to him the question: "Simon, do you love me?" (Jn. 21,15ff.). The solemn threefold declaration is intended to give legal force to the transmission of authority. The significant thing is that the love of Peter appears as the prerequisite for him to be commissioned to feed the flock of Jesus Christ. The transmission of authority presupposes union with the risen Lord, and in a special sense. This is not only a subjective norm but an ontological spiritual one. Those who exercise spiritual authority must live in the peace of God and in peace with their brothers. They live in the sphere of activity of the Holy Spirit, of the salvific power of Jesus Christ.

On the other hand the Church, in the course of her history, was forced to arrive at the realization that the required union with Christ can be lacking without the papal authority thereby being forfeited. This was stated specifically against the theses of Wyclif, Hus, and Luther. The primacy would indeed be a perishable thing if it were dependent, for better or worse, on the disposition of the individual pope. Since Jesus Christ is invisible and the thoughts and feelings of the human heart are hidden, it can never be determined with certainty whether and to what extent a man lives in the faith of Jesus Christ. When we see in history how Christ tolerates and is patient with a sinful, faithless representative, and continues to use as an instrument one who has fallen away from him, we face a deep mystery. Here the anger of God, still active in the Church despite the final saving revelation, assumes its most awful dimension. But it is precisely here that the disturbing mystery reveals itself, that this authority is of God, or Jesus Christ, who acts through men, and that consequently we are not dependent on the holiness or unholiness of a man, but on God alone, who can make use of both sinners and saints to communicate himself.

The sacramentality of the papacy is rooted concretely in the fact that the pope is, and always must be, a bishop; that is, that he possesses the highest of the sacred orders in the Church. It cannot be maintained, against this thesis, that the pope immediately after his election is in possession of full ecclesiastical power, even when he is not yet a bishop or priest, and therefore receives the consecration as bishop only after his election. The election and the episcopal consecration are inseparably connected, forming an organic if not necessarily a temporal unity. As far as the power of orders is concerned, the pope, it is true, is not superior to the other bishops; but the power of orders is not the immediate ground of his supreme authority. His supreme authority rests, rather, on the ground that as bishop of Rome he is the successor of Peter. So even if his power of orders does not exceed that of the other bishops, we may still say that for the eye of faith, it is in the pope's consecrated power that the sacramental character of the entire Church is made visible.

We can trace this connection still more explicitly. Christ transmitted the power of his own mission to his apostles and their successors. This was a single power, but in the course of time as a result of the needs of the Church it separated into two parts, the power of orders and the power of jurisdiction. The two are spoken of separately in the exercise of the bishop's office, but there remains in each of them something of the original unity and singleness of the power. The power of orders contains an element of the shepherd's office, and in the power of jurisdiction there is more to be seen than a merely juridical authority; it includes a sanctifying component.

PRIMACY AND EPISCOPACY

The universal episcopacy of the pope raises the question of the relation of the primacy to the episcopacy. The question is important, when we recall that the First Vatican Council calls the papal power a true episcopal power. Notwithstanding the division of the Church into bishoprics, the pope is universal bishop, so that the entire Church appears as one bishopric. Although the pope is not any higher than the other bishops as far as the power of orders is concerned, he is nevertheless, in his power of jurisdiction and in his primatial authority, bishop over all the members of the church, over the bishops and the other faithful. He can make use of this episcopal authority over everyone in the Church. This does not mean, however, that there are two bishops in every diocese, the local bishop and the universal bishop. Despite the pope's direct episcopal power, the local bishop remains the immediate shepherd of the flock entrusted to him. The relationship of the pope's universal episcopal power to that of the local bishop cannot be encompassed in a satisfactory juridical formula. It can be stated, however, that the universal episcopal power does not justify the pope's interference at will. "The right of the pope to intervene in the administration of a diocese does not rest on an equal and concurrent competence with the ordinary of the diocese, but rather on a higher right, which may only be exercised in accord with the principle of subsidiarity, when the ordinary agency fails" (K. Mörsdorf).

POPE AND CHURCH

For the one in office the primacy has a binding character. The pope is not free to do as he pleases. He is not free to be silent when he must speak, nor to speak when he must keep silence. However much depends on his judgment, and must so depend, still he is inescapably bound to the commission of Jesus Christ. This commission means service to the People of God and to the salvation of each individual. The pope is in office as a member of the Church and for the Church. The pope's action derives from the Church and also serves the Church. Pope and Church are not as two things coming together from outside and encountering each other. The pope speaks as a member of the Church—a member endowed with the highest authority—speaking to the other members, who in their turn form a fraternal community with him in their midst as father and brother. So, although the primacy is the highest authority, its whole meaning is committed service.

The pope is responsible to Christ for this service to the salvation of all. The primacy is meant to be an expression of love, of that love which acts in the service of man, in obedience to God's eternal plan of salvation. What Paul proclaims in the thirteenth chapter of First Corinthians also applies here, namely that all gifts in the Church are fruitless unless their soul is love. "There are three things that last forever, faith, hope, and love; but the greatest of them all is love" (1 Cor. 13,13). But the love which is meant here is of such a kind that it cannot simply be an affirmation or confirmation of men in their self-confidence or in corrupt worldliness; rather, it calls them from pride and self-seeking to the freedom of the children of God, from anxiety to peace. Frequently this means conflict and perturbation for a man; he shrinks from this surrender to God, finding the demand too great. So for him a service of love becomes a scandal.

These considerations also show that the exercise of the primacy has its measure, its limits, and its necessity in the sovereignty of God and the salvation of men. The primacy cannot be an exercise in obedience for the sake of obedience; the obedience must lead to Christ by the way of love. Since man's freedom is his highest natural good and in doubtful cases has the priority, representing an analogy to the freedom of God, the papacy must not limit this freedom in a greater degree than is necessary for salvation.

◄ 20

Papal Infallibility

THE INFALLIBILITY OF LOVE

Infallibility is a special form of the sovereign papal power. The meaning of the infallibility ascribed to the pope must first of all be made clear: it means that he proclaims the Christian revelation authentically, without substantial misconception. Its basis is found in the infallibility of the whole Church, as was clearly stated by the First as well as the Second Vatican Council. When the Second Vatican Council, repeating what the Council of Trent had already said, gives to the proclamation of the word of God the precedence over all the other tasks of the Church, then the revelation of Jesus Christ handed down by the apostolic Church is made of primary importance. The People of God received the inheritance of revelation from the apostles, to be safeguarded faithfully and announced to all men, that it might shape in faith, hope, and charity the life of each individual, as well as that of the community, until the second coming of Jesus Christ. The People of God would not be the People of God, nor the Body of Christ, were it to believe anything other than what had been said by Jesus Christ and handed down by the apostles. It is nourished constantly by the body and blood of the Lord, and it lives forever in true confession of him and of his Father. This confession confirms every salvific word and deed of Jesus and seeks an ever deeper understanding of them. Here the unity of the People of God shows itself as a unity in faith, which is a visible manifestation of the sacramental community. "The members of God's People communicate with one another in the same Christ-faith, because they communicate with Christ."

Christ himself gave to the Church the task of proclaiming the gospel (Mt. 28,18–20; Mk. 16,15.20; Lk. 24,47–49). It is a chief element of the mission which the Church received from her Lord (Jn. 20,21). Thus Jesus can identify the teaching authority of the disciples with his own (Lk. 10,16), and in order to fulfill this teaching mission, he who came into the world to give true witness (Jn. 18,37) will remain present until the end of time (Mt. 16,18; 28,20; Lk. 22,31f.). Further, he promises the Church the Holy Spirit, who will establish her in all truth. He will not speak of himself, but what he hears he will speak, and what is coming he will make known (Jn. 14,16; 15,26; 16,12f.). He will take care that nothing is forgotten, for he will constantly recall the Church to what she has received from her Lord (Jn. 14,26; 16,13f.). He will not speak anything new, but rather interpret what has been said and so make it appear in its fullness. In the power of the Holy Spirit the Church can and will give witness to Jesus Christ, who is her Lord and her Messiah (Lk. 24,49; Jn. 15,26; Acts 1,8). The disciples will preach from the housetops what Jesus has spoken to them in secret (Mt. 10,27). To hear their message is the same as to hear Christ himself (Lk. 10,16; Mt. 10,40). Therefore those who hear the preaching of the Church and embrace it will be saved; those who reject it will be lost (Mk. 16,16). Through the Holy Spirit the Church is sanctified for the truth until the end of time (Jn. 17,17ff.). For this reason the disciples must demand unconditional faith and obedience for the word of their proclamation. Their message admits of no restrictions and no reservations (Acts 14,19; 2 Tim. 2,9). It is not the word of man but of God, although in human form (2 Cor. 4,5; 1 Thess. 2,13). They accomplish the word of their proclamation on the order of Jesus (Rom. 10,17; 1 Cor. 9,15), as the service of the Word and of the salvation of man (Acts 1, 2ff.; Eph. 4,14). The Holy Spirit guarantees the dependability and integrity of the proclamation (Acts 5,32; 15,2; cf. 1 Cor. 7,25; Rom. 1,1; 2,16; 2 Thess. 1,8; Gal. 1,11f.; 1,16; Titus 1,9). The Church is thus the pillar of truth (1 Tim. 3,15).

In the ancient Church the faith was expressed in the liturgy, in the reports of the sayings and deeds of Jesus; it was put into confessional and faith formulas, not to be changed with the times. All these together formed the rule of faith. According to Irenaeus, the Church is a rich treasury in which the truth handed down by the apostles is guarded and preserved in its undiminished fullness (*Against the False Gnosis*, III,4,1). In the great councils the Church would render service to the truth of Jesus Christ by an authentic and dynamic proclamation against threatening dangers to the faith. In this self-understanding of the Church there was the conviction that the People of God as such, in its faith in Christ and its preaching of him, is infallible. The theology of the Middle Ages was filled with the same conviction. Thomas Aquinas, for example, says: "The universal Church cannot err" (*Summa Theologica*, II, q. la, art. 2.10; quodlibitum ix, q. 1, art. 7).

PAPAL INFALLIBILITY AS GUARANTEE FOR THE CHURCH'S INFALLIBILITY

Because of its societal composition, which is inherent in the Church as a historical, real society and which was foreseen by Christ and realized by the Holy Spirit, the community of faith becomes visible in the Church's representatives; that is to say, in the college of bishops with the pope at its head. But it is just this relationship of the episcopal college (the council) to the pope which becomes a problem. The debate precipitated by Wyclif and Hus and the threat presented by the Great Western Schism aggravated the question as to who within the Church is the infallible teaching authority and what the conditions are for an infallible proclamation. The consciousness of the authenticity of the Church's faith and the Church's word, associated in the ancient Church with the operation of the Holy Spirit and the active presence of Christ and therefore with the sacramental dimension, came to be more and more a juridical consideration. In this development the matter of the pope's infallibility came prominently into the foreground. The question received new impetus in modern times through Gallicanism, Febronianism, and Conciliarism. In the centuries'-long debate, the understanding was reached that the pope, insofar as he is the representative of the whole Church, always possesses the highest authority in the Church. So the infallibility of the Church manifests itself in the infallibility of the pope. His supreme authority to teach is a special element in his sovereign power to rule. This was defined by the First Vatican Council.

As the power to teach is to be considered part of the sovereign ruling power, it does not constitute a third power along with the power of orders and the power of jurisdiction. It remains within the two powers, which are realized at different times in a variety of ways. Insofar as the teaching authority of the pope—that is, his competence to determine the content of revelation with certainty—serves the proclamation of the gospel and is not simply a matter of scholarly knowledge and the statement of truth, insofar therefore as it is exercised for the sake of salvation, it has an inner relation to the power of sanctification. For the proclamation is the communication of the Church's salvific activity. In the preaching of the Church, God himself communicates himself in words to the hearers. The certainty of the Church's proclamation, based on the pope's infallibility, provides the guarantee for the authenticity of the Church's faith and its preaching. The force of history, which brings in its course constant change and continual reversal and renewal, makes it logical and even imperative that in the Church as the People of God—notwithstanding the fact that it is a society existing in history—the word of revelation once communicated should neither be lost nor changed in its essential content. Because Jesus Christ himself was solicitously aware of this situation, he provided that the Holy Spirit should be the life principle of the Church. Although the Spirit manifests his activity in a variety of ways and is not exclusively bound or restricted to the canonical offices, nevertheless in the actions of the officials his operation appears in a tangible, concrete, historical form.

THE MEANING OF THE DOCTRINE

The unity and certainty of the faith of God's People is closely related to papal infallibility. This appears very clearly in the chief text in which the Church sets forth this doctrine (Decrees of the First Vatican Council, third session, ch. 4, DS 3065–3074):

This Holy See has always held that the supreme power of teaching is also included in this apostolic primacy which the Roman Pontiff, as the successor of St. Peter, the Prince of the Apostles, holds over the whole Church. The perpetual practice of the Church confirms this; and the ecumenical councils have declared it, especially those in which the Eastern and Western Churches were united in faith and love.

For the Fathers of the Fourth Council of Constantinople, following closely in the footsteps of their predecessors, made this solemn profession: "The first condition of salvation is to keep the norm of the true faith. For it is impossible that the words of our Lord Jesus Christ who said, 'Thou art Peter, and upon this rock I will build my Church' (Mt. 16,18), should not be verified. And their truth has been proved by the course of history, for in the Apostolic See the Catholic religion has always been kept unsullied, and its teaching kept holy. From this faith and doctrine we by no means desire to be separated; and we hope that we may deserve to be associated with you in the one communion which the Apostolic See proclaims, in which the whole, true and perfect security of the Christian religion resides."

Furthermore, with the approval of the Second Council of Lyons, the Greeks professed "that the holy Roman Church has supreme and full primacy and jurisdiciton over the whole Catholic Church. This it truly and humbly recognizes as received from the Lord himself in the person of St. Peter, the Prince or head of the Apostles, whose successor in the fullness of power is the Roman Pontiff. And just as the holy Roman Church is bound more than all the others to defend the truth of faith, so, if there arise any questions concerning the faith, they must be decided by its judgment."

Finally, the Council of Florence defined "that the Roman Pontiff is the true vicar of Christ, the head of the whole Church, the father and teacher of all Christians; and that to him, in the person of St. Peter, was given by our Lord Jesus Christ the full power of feeding, ruling, and governing the whole Church."

To satisfy this pastoral duty, Our predecessors have always expended untiring effort to propagate Christ's doctrine of salvation among all the peoples of the world. And with similar care they have watched that the doctrine might be preserved genuine and pure wherever it was received. Therefore, the bishops of the whole world, sometimes singly, sometimes assembled in councils, following the long-standing custom of the churches and the form of the ancient rule, reported to this Apostolic See those dangers especially which came up in matters of faith, so that here where the faith can suffer no diminution, the harm suffered by the faith might be repaired. However, the Roman Pontiffs on their part, according as the condition of the times and the circumstances dictated, sometimes calling together ecumenical councils or sounding out the mind of the Church throughout the whole world, sometimes through regional councils, or sometimes by using other helps which divine Providence supplied, have, with the help of God, defined as to be held such matters as they had found consonant with the Holy Scripture and with the apostolic tradition. The reason for this is not that the Holy Spirit was promised to the successors of St. Peter that they might make known new doctrine by his revelation, but rather, that, with his assistance, they might jealously guard and faithfully explain the revelation or deposit of faith that was handed down through the apostles. Indeed, it was this apostolic doctrine that all the Fathers held, and the holy orthodox Doctors reverenced and followed. For they fully realized that this See of St. Peter always remains untainted by any error, according to the divine promise of our Lord and Savior made to the prince of his disciples, "I have prayed for thee, that thy faith may not fail; and do thou, when once thou hast turned again, strengthen thy brethren (Lk. 22,32)."

Now this charism of truth and of never-failing faith was conferred upon St. Peter and his successors in this Chair, in order that they might perform their supreme office for the salvation of all; that by them the whole flock of Christ might be kept away from the poison of error and be nourished by the food of heavenly doctrine; that the occasion of schism might be removed, the whole Church preserved as one, and secure on its foundation, stand firm against the gates of hell.

But since in this present age, which especially requires the salutary efficacy of the apostolic office, not a few are found who minimize its authority, We think it extremely necessary to assert solemnly the prerogative which the only-begotten Son of God deigned to join to the highest pastoral office.

And so, faithfully keeping to the tradition received from the beginning of the Christian faith, for the glory of God our Savior, for the exaltation of the Catholic religion, and for the salvation of Christian peoples, We, with the approval of the sacred council, teach and define that it is a divinely revealed dogma: that the Roman Pontiff, when he speaks *ex cathedra*, that is, when, acting in the office of shepherd and teacher of all Christians, he defines, by virtue of his supreme apostolic authority, doctrine concerning faith or morals to be held by the universal Church, possesses through the divine assistance promised to him in the person of St. Peter, the infallibility with which the divine Redeemer willed his Church to be endowed in defining doctrine concerning faith or morals;

and that such definitions of the Roman Pontiff are therefore irreformable because of their nature, but not because of the agreement of the Church.

In interpreting the statement of the First Vatican Council it must be remembered that because of the polemic involved in the resistance to the conciliar theory, the infallibility of the pope was stressed with extraordinary forcefulness. The ancient belief in the infallibility of the entire Church is not forgotten in this text: it states explicitly that the pope possesses that infallibility with which the divine Savior would see his Church provided. But although it was the council which defined infallibly the infallibility of the pope, very little is made of the infallibility of the council. The connection of the pope's infallibility with the Church as a whole appears only as a minor element. In particular, the infallibility belonging to the episcopal college with the pope at its head is not brought out explicitly or with fitting emphasis. The phrase "such definitions are irreformable because of their nature, but not because of the agreement of the Church" (not *ex consensu ecclesiae*) appears to put unusual stess on the isolation of the pope over against the entire Church, so that misunderstanding could arise to the effect that the pope could define a dogma contrary to the faith of the Church and impose it against the Church's will.

THE FIRST VATICAN COUNCIL AND THE SECOND

The Second Vatican Council filled in the gap left by this one-sided emphasis on infallibility in several ways. It is noticeable, first of all, that Vatican II prefers the word "proclamation" (preaching) to the word "dogma" (teaching), and this has the effect of giving the Council's statements a less juridical and a more sacramental tone. Dogma as function of the teaching office is not disregarded. However, it was brought out more clearly than by Vatican I that dogma derives its meaning from proclamation and is a help to proclamation. Moreover Vatican II placed the doctrine of papal infallibility within the context of the infallibility of the universal Church or that of the episcopal college presided over by the pope. The decisive text of Vatican II is as follows (Constitution on the Church, #25):

Although the individual bishops do not enjoy the prerogative of infallibility, they can nevertheless proclaim Christ's doctrine infallibly. This is so, even when they are dispersed around the world, provided that while maintaining the bond of unity among themselves and with Peter's successor, and while teaching authentically on a matter of faith or morals, they concur in a single viewpoint as the one which must be held conclusively. This authority is even more clearly verified when, gathered together in an ecumenical council, they are teachers and judges of faith and morals for the universal Church. Their definitions must then be adhered to with the submission of faith.

This infallibility with which the divine Redeemer willed His Church to be endowed in defining a doctrine of faith and morals extends as far as the deposit of divine revelation, which must be religiously guarded and faithfully expounded. This is the infallibility which the Roman Pontiff, the head of the college of bishops, enjoys in virtue of his office, when, as the supreme shepherd and teacher of all the faithful, who confirms his brethren in their faith (cf. Lk. 22,32), he proclaims by a definitive act some doctrine of faith or morals. Therefore his definitions, of themselves, and not from the consent of the Church, are justly styled irreformable, for they are pronounced with the assistance of the Holy Spirit, an assistance promised to him in blessed Peter. Therefore they need no approval of others, nor do they allow an appeal to any other judgment. For then the Roman Pontiff is not pronouncing judgment as a private person. Rather, as the supreme teacher of the universal Church, as one in whom the charism of the infallibility of the Church herself is individually present, he is expounding or defending a doctrine of Catholic faith.

The infallibility promised to the Church resides also in the body of bishops when that body exercises supreme teaching authority with the successor of Peter. To the resultant definitions the assent of the Church can never be wanting, on account of the activity of that same Holy Spirit, whereby the whole flock of Christ is preserved and progresses in unity of faith.

Twice in this text the infallibility of the universal Church is brought out prominently. It would not be true to the sense of the text to distinguish between an active infallibility on the part of those who hold the teaching office and a passive infallibility on the part of the hearers. In a certain sense all members of the Church share passively in the infallibility, for they are all receivers of the divine truth. They are all hearers: faith comes by hearing. But in a broader and far different sense all those belonging to the Church participate actively in the infallibility, insofar as they are all called to give witness to Jesus Christ. Vatican II takes this into account when it says the following (Constitution on the Church, #12):

> The holy People of God shares also in Christ's prophetic office. It spreads abroad a living witness to Him, especially by means of a life of faith and charity; and by offering to God a sacrifice of praise, the tribute of lips which give honor to His name (cf. Heb. 13,15). The body of the faithful as a whole, anointed as they are by the Holy One (cf. Jn. 2,20.27), cannot err in matters of belief. Thanks to a supernatural sense of the faith which characterizes the People as a whole, it manifests this unerring quality when, "from the bishops down to the last member of the laity," it shows universal agreement in matters of faith and morals.
>
> For, by this sense of faith which is aroused and sustained by the Spirit of truth, God's People accepts not the word of men but the very Word of God (cf. 1 Thess. 2,13). It clings without fail to the faith once delivered to the saints (cf. Jude 3), penetrates it more deeply by accurate insights, and applies it more thoroughly to life. All this it does under the lead of a sacred teaching authority to which it loyally defers.

INFALLIBLE DEFINITIONS AND THE LIFE OF THE CHURCH

The organic connection between papal infallibility and the life of the whole Church is this: when the pope speaks infallibly in defining a doctrine, he is speaking as the head of the episcopal college; and, inasmuch as the bishops are representatives of the local churches and at the same time, in their collegiality, of the universal Church, he represents the universal Church. From above he represents Jesus Christ; from below he represents the whole Church. As Christ's representative he speaks to the People of God of whom he is himself a member. As representative of the Church he proclaims in its name that faith which is both his and theirs. In his word the faith of the community receives a concrete form in history.

An infallible pronouncement of the pope may have the character of a doctrine for instruction, but it has also the nature of a confession of Christ. It is the Church presenting itself as a community of believers in Christ, and doing this through the representative appointed by him. The pope is the speaker for the community. So an infallible definition of the pope is a self-fulfillment of the People of God as the Body of Jesus Christ. It is reasonable therefore, as the Second Vatican Council has said, that assent cannot be wanting to such a papal pronouncement, which is a confession of faith in Jesus Christ made in the name of the entire People. It cannot be wanting because the pope's confession of Christ is the confession of the People of God, and therefore every member of this People finds himself in the confession of the pope. As head of the community the pope is the speaker for that community.

Of course, very few papal statements make a claim to infallibility; indeed the greatest part of the pope's utterances make no such claim. According to the prevailing opinion of theologians, papal encyclicals (e.g., *Humani Generis* of Pius XII), addresses, letters on matters of faith, belong to this class of statements which are not presented as infallible. To such papal statements the Catholic will not be indifferent; but if he should reach the final, undoubting conviction that a papal pronouncement is not in accord with divine revelation, he will face the difficult question of conscience of how his conviction of the truth, on the one hand, is to be reconciled with his regard for the faith community of the Church, on the other.

THE SCOPE OF PAPAL INFALLIBILITY

According to statements of both the First and Second Vatican Councils, the scope of papal infallibility comprehends the whole of the Christian revelation. The pope and the college of bishops must adhere to this; it is the norm for all their statements. "All are obliged to maintain and be ruled by this revelation, which, as written or preserved by tradition, is transmitted in its entirety through the legitimate succession of bishops and especially through the care of the Roman Pontiff himself" (Constitution on the Church, #25). However, one must also include in the sphere of papal infallibility those areas which, either as presuppositions or as consequences, are so closely related to the area of revelation that the latter itself does not remain safe when these former are not also assured. Included in this principle is the corollary that the pope is called upon to speak definitively in the field of natural law—difficult though this is to define—inasmuch as it is closely related to revelation and the salvation of man. It must also lie within his province to decide whether such a relationship exists. Many times, in order to determine this, very basic and extensive studies are necessary in areas which can only be handled by experts in the field. The difficulty here is exemplified by the case of Galileo, or in the birth control issue. Despite this difficulty the problem cannot be done away with. Exact theological limits for an area cannot be ascertained with any absolute certainty, and up to the present day they have not been so determined by theologians. Furthermore, it may be that this is not absolutely necessary, because in the case of faith, unlike other knowledge, it is not a question of right or wrong theories, but, in the last analysis, of a surrender to Jesus Christ in the area of those truths which have been made clear by him.

Of course it cannot be overlooked that this field has a center, namely, Jesus Christ himself; and from this center lines run as radii to a circumference which cannot be precisely described. We are nevertheless able to say of certain pronouncements that they lie within this realm of faith or outside it.

LIMITS OF THE DOCTRINE OF INFALLIBILITY

The word "infallibility" requires further limitation. It is a word of rather unhappy origins, having derived from a declining Scholasticism, which has prevailed since the Council of Trent. We should completely misapprehend what the Church means by it if we were to identify infallibility with perfection or complete fulfillment—to say nothing of personal sinlessness! But that such misconceptions are possible need not be stressed; when it is not clearly defined it sounds presumptuous and overbearing. In its positive sense, the expression states that the legacy of salvation left by Christ, the saving truth handed down from the apostles, is preserved and presented by the Church as authentic and trustworthy. "Infallible" definitions of faith are signs of the profound and solemn earnestness with which the Church fulfills her responsibility in relation to Christ, her Lord present in the Spirit.

No explanation of infallibility can be concluded without noting that faith pronouncements are subject to that law which Paul once expressed: "For our knowledge and our prophecy alike are partial, and the partial vanishes when wholeness comes. . . . Now we see only puzzling reflections in a mirror, but then we shall see face to face. My knowledge now is partial; then it will be whole, like God's knowledge of me." (1 Cor. 13,9–12) This means that the mode of a statement of faith, insofar as time, place, and language have their bearing on its formulation, shares in the relativity of the historical. It should further be emphasized that the formula is conditioned in its reception by personal idiosyncrasies, strengths and failings, partialities, tolerances and intolerances on the part of those whom it affects. Finally, it must also be realized that such faith decisions share in the general eschatological character of the Church and their full meaning relates to the end of time. They are clarifications in a particular area of faith in the face of some threat or present danger. Nevertheless the definition constitutes a beginning rather than an end, for it is a challenge to a deeper understanding not only of the truth defined but also of its place and its value within the whole of Christian revelation.

Since the form of the definition is closely bound up with the situation in which it is proclaimed, it is clear that with the advance of culture and the development of the scope of human language and knowledge, the dogma experiences a linguistic embodiment which is always new. Moreover, owing to the connection between form and content, the new embodiment will lead to an understanding of the faith which is always more comprehensive and thorough and sometimes more nuanced and synthesized.

For the proper execution of his teaching authority the pope must concern himself with the understanding of divine revelation. The charism of infallibility does not free him from this responsibility, for although it is true that the Holy Spirit protects him from error, it is not by a process of direct enlightenment. The means to an understanding of revelation are of many kinds: scientific and prescientific studies, dialogue with non-Catholic

Christian Churches, with the non-Christian religions, with atheism, and with the cultural, philosophical, and scholarly movements of the times. In purely secular matters the pope can lay claim to no direct power. (The claims of some popes in the Middle Ages were conditioned by the times; they were the outgrowth of political developments, not the natural flowering of Christ's endowment to his Church.) But in the spiritual sphere he has the assistance of the Holy Spirit which is given him as a constitutive element of his office. He must exercise the power received from Christ within the world, and therefore he must take a position with respect to the events occurring within the world of the faithful. It is his right and his duty to measure the events of history against the law of Jesus Christ.

Index

DOGMA ➤ *Volume 4: The Church*

A PROJECT OF JOHN XXIII INSTITUTE
Saint Xavier College, Chicago

Edited by T. Patrick Burke